Changing Lives

More stories from London's Little Italy

© Camden History Society
and the Estate of Olive Besagni

ISBN 978 0904491 95 1

Two views of the annual Italian Procession; arrowed: Carmine Grieco (p 12)

Changing Lives
More stories from London's Little Italy

Olive Besagni

Compiled by Olive Besagni, née Ferrari
Edited by David A Hayes
Designed by Ivor Kamlish

Preface

This collection of oral histories is a sequel to A Better Life, likewise compiled by Olive Besagni and published by Camden History Society in 2011. Since its launch, A Better Life has been the Society's best-selling publication. It tells of Italian families who, from the early 19th century onwards, escaped from rural poverty in Italy and emigrated to London in search of a better life, settling amid the slums of Clerkenwell.

The neighbourhood they colonised became variously known as 'The Italian Quarter' or 'Little Italy ', while its inhabitants affectionately referred to it as 'The Hill'. (Back Hill, sloping down from Clerkenwell Road into the valley of the long-buried River Fleet, is one of the area's main thoroughfares.) After World War II many Italian families left the largely redeveloped area, resettling in the suburbs or beyond. But St Peter's Italian Church remains to this day today a focus of spiritual and social life for Italians across London – this never more apparent than during the Italian Procession each summer.

In Olive's second book the emphasis is more is on the descendants of the original immigrants, the lives they made for themselves in Clerkenwell and their experiences in the changing world of the twentieth century. The text had been completed when, sadly, in December 2016 Olive passed away at the age of 91. Her family were most keen that publication of her work should go ahead, and I am grateful for their help in finalising the copy at a difficult time for them; particular thanks are due to Olive's husband Bruno, son Tony and daughters Nicky and Anita. Olive would undoubtedly have wished to extend her own heartfelt thanks to all those who contributed their memories and precious family photos.

Little Italy, as defined in the book, straddles the modern borough boundary between Camden and Islington. Camden History Society is nonetheless proud to publish this book, both for its further invaluable insights into the area's past, and in memory of its remarkable author.

David Hayes,
Editor, Camden History Society publications

Contents

Introduction	6
The Wrong Country (Cicco family)	8
Rosa Lusardi	15
Joe Bacuzzi – 'the Legend'	18
Charles Nolan's reminiscences	20
Silvio Giovanelli	24
Victor Kibble's reminiscences	27
Lebaldi and his tortoises	31
Peter Bertoncini	32
Mario Fabrizi – the comic actor	34
The Mazzini-Garibaldi Club	35
The annual Scampagnata	37
Pieces by Achille Pompa	
'Little Italy's lost art and artistes'	39
'Steamboat Serenade'	40
'Buckingham Palace'	41
'St Peter's Italian Church'	41
Angelo Carlo Dainese, inventor	43
St Peter's School: diary extracts	45
Miranda Sedgewick, née Franchi	48
Mamie Secchi	50
The Fratellanza Club fracas	52
Easter in the Hill	53
Two well-loved priests	55
A changing world – Delia's story	58
Runnymede 1944-1949	61
Afterword	64
Olive Besagni – what a life!	65
Index	70

Introduction by Olive Besagni

This is my second book, a sequel to A Better Life in which I told the stories of Italian immigrants arriving in Clerkenwell, London and settling in what became known as 'The Italian Quarter', or 'Little Italy', an area set in the triangle of streets between Clerkenwell Road, Rosebery Avenue and Farringdon Road. These migrants left their homes in the valleys and mountain ranges of Northern Italy, where in many cases they had been living in abject poverty, their homes nothing more than barns, with no sanitation. Their family, if they had one, would no doubt have been very unhappy to see their sons or daughters leave for what in many instances was an unknown destination. There would have been great sorrow, but needs must, they had to go forth.

At the time of writing, I am still stunned by the amazing reception that my first book received. I had had no idea of the popularity of its subject, the story of the Italian immigrants who have now integrated almost silently into the English way of life whilst maintaining their own culture and love of their homeland. I can claim to understand how they feel on account of my own background. My mother, Jeanetta Oxley, was English, from a family of business people who owned ironmonger shops across the country, from the Midlands to London, where they manufactured saws, and sold everything from scissors to roller skates, and zinc baths of all sizes.

My father, Giuseppe Ferrari, of Italian descent and born in the Italian Quarter of Clerkenwell, was quite well off. Over several decades from 1880, his own father, Giovanni Ferrari, was the headmaster of St Peter's Italian School. Having taught in Italy, my grandfather had been transferred to England by the Italian government. At St Peter's he taught Italian grammar to the immigrants who were then illiterate, almost without exception.

At the start of the twentieth century, whole families began to arrive in Clerkenwell, consisting mostly of Northern Italians, whose antecedents had already made the journey to London. Very early travellers had suffered many hardships on their journey to England, many of them had walked all the way from their homes. These families were preceded by young men travelling alone and there is no doubt that their journeys were hazardous. One saving grace was that the life they had led in the mountain regions they had left behind would have made them self-sufficient in providing themselves with a meal of dandelion leaves or nettles, mushrooms or chestnuts, depending on the season. But, when they passed through the cities and small towns they would have been unable to afford any of the good things on offer there. Crossing the Channel from Calais and other ports in Northern France would often prove to be a major problem. The regular steamer services would be unaffordable to many, but those who had managed to earn a little money on their way across Europe, could doubtless have made a deal to cross the Channel in one way or another, perhaps on a small craft or a fishing vessel. And many a frightened stowaway was found cowering in the hold of boats bound for England.

One fare-paying passenger was Salvatore Cicco, whose family is the subject of our first story.

Olive signing copies of A Better Life on a stall at the Italian Procession

The Wrong Country

**The Cicco family's story,
as told to Olive Besagni in 2013
by Tony Grieco**

Salvatore Cicco disembarked from the S.S. Hawarden Castle on 11 September 1896. It was a somewhat dank and foggy evening. This surprised him because he had been told that the climate of Buenos Aires was similar to that of his home town of Naples. He was even more surprised when he found that he had not arrived in Argentina but was in London. A mix up at the ticket office, combined with his total lack of knowledge of the English language, had resulted in Salvatore's emigrating to the wrong country. After the initial shock, he decided that this mistake did not make that much difference to his general plan. England may not have been his first choice but he would try his luck here anyway.

Salvatore Cicco

Raffaela Cicco

Salvatore was born in Naples in 1867. He had married Raffaela D'Anna, from Nola, and by 1896 they had a young son Giuseppe. Salvatore was a cabinet maker by trade, but a lack of opportunity in Italy had persuaded him to seek his fortune abroad. He left Raffaela and Giuseppe back in Nola with a promise that, if he established himself, he would send for them within 18 months. Failing that, he would return to Italy.

That first night in London Salvatore found lodgings at an Italian café close to where he had landed at London Bridge. The next morning the café owner's son took him to the Italian Church in Clerkenwell, where he explained his situation. The priests found him a place in one of the many lodging houses 'down the Hill', and sent him to a number of local workshops owned by Italians to find work.

Those early days were hard. Salvatore was separated from his wife and family. He was in a strange land where he didn't even understand the language, but at least he had the company and support of fellow countrymen. He was a good craftsman and he worked hard. He was not a drinker or a gambler and within a year he had saved enough to send for his wife and child as he had promised.

The Cicco family

Over the next few years Salvatore and his growing family lived and worked around the streets of the *Quartiere Italiano*. They moved fairly frequently as the family grew. Between 1897 and 1915 they had six or seven children, although only five survived infancy: Antonio (Tony), Anna (Annie), Felice (Phil), Maria (Mary) and Concetta (Connie). In that time they had lived in Eyre Street Hill, Summer Street, Bakers Row and Victoria Dwellings.

All the boys followed in their father's footsteps and became cabinet makers. Mr Taylor, the headmaster of St Peter's School, pushed very hard for Giuseppe (known as Joe) to stay on in school and take a scholarship, but Salvatore said he needed his eldest son to start working for the family as soon as he was able. In the old-fashioned Italian way, the girls stayed at home to help their mother. Annie was quiet and reserved; Mary was more outgoing and playful. Both were excellent cooks in the homely Italian style.

When Italy joined the Allies in the First World War, Joe went off to join the Italian Army, because he had been born in Italy. Salvatore decided that Tony should go with his brother, even though Tony had been born in London. This caused a little difficulty when Tony was eventually called up to join the British Army. However, the fact that he had

Tony and Joe in uniform

volunteered for the Italian Army well before his British call up saved him from being labelled an avoider, and as the two countries were allies there was no further trouble.

Both brothers were fortunate in their wartime experiences. Tony was sent to work as a hospital orderly and was in the relative safety of a behind the lines hospital for all of his service. Joe did serve in a combat unit and saw active service on the Austrian Front. He was a corporal in the 35th Regiment and was decorated. He avoided any wounds but was hospitalised for a while with malaria, which then affected him for the rest of his life. In 1917 the reverses suffered by the Italian Army led to large numbers of British troops being sent to reinforce the Italian Front. Having spent almost all his life in London, Joe was soon posted as an interpreter and spent the rest of the war attached to a battalion of the Royal Warwickshire Regiment. This was to prove fortunate over 20 years later during WWII when, after Mussolini sided with Hitler. Italians in London were interned. Despite being an Italian citizen, a member of the Italian Ex-Servicemen's Association and a member of the Mazzini-Garibaldi club, Joe avoided internment because of that attachment to the British Army in WWI.

Joe with the Royal Warwickshire Regiment, seated second from left in second row

The years between 1918 and 1930 were to prove very successful for the Cicco family. Salvatore set up his own cabinet-making business, with a workshop in Albion Street (now Balfe Street) at King's Cross. He had his three sons working with him and even employed two or three other workers. The business mostly produced reproduction antique furniture for stores such as Maple's. Joe was a good designer and some more modern pieces were also produced. Tony married at this time. In the true old-fashioned Italian style, he went to Italy to find a bride and married Rosa Abate from San Paolo Bel Sito, a little village outside Nola. Tony left the family business to work in parquet floor laying and to bring up his own family. He had three sons, Salvatore (known as Cyril), Rafaele (Ray) and Emilio. The other brothers remained unmarried.

This period of growing prosperity was not to last. By the early 1920s Raffaela was finding it increasingly difficult to walk or even stand comfortably. Visits to doctors and specialists proved fruitless (and expensive). Various cures and procedures were tried with no success. Salvatore took his wife for a prolonged stay in Italy, hoping that the warmer climate might prove helpful. Despite the nine months in Nola, Raffaela's condition got worse and even a pilgrimage to Lourdes brought no amelioration of her condition. By 1930 she was virtually bedridden. From the description of her symptoms and progress of the condition, it seems likely that she was suffering from a form of multiple sclerosis. His wife's illness had exhausted Salvatore, physically and financially. In June 1931 he died and the business closed.

The family moved back to Clerkenwell and took two flats in Cavendish Mansions, Clerkenwell Road. Joe and Phil continued working in the cabinet-making trade, while Anna and Mary took what jobs they could while looking after their mother. Neither of them married. Mary had a couple of proposals but always told the prospective suitors that she had a duty to the rest of the family, and that she wouldn't leave her mother. Raffaela died in 1948.

Tony, Rosa and his family had lived in Clerkenwell in the 1930s and 1940s and the three grandsons were frequent visitors to their nonna. The 'Boys' (as they were always known even when in their fifties) were played with and teased by their aunts, particularly Mary who was always a playful and kindly character. Tony eventually moved the family to Holloway. His sons grew into tall strong young men, taking after their grandfather Salvatore. Tony suffered from a weak heart and died in 1958, followed by his wife Rosa only a month later. In keeping with her nature, Mary immediately gave up her job and went to look after the 'Boys', now in their twenties but not yet married. She stayed until they had settled down. Cyril married first, then Ray and finally Emilio.

Salvatore's youngest daughter, Connie, would always say she was spoiled as a child. She grew up during the period of relative prosperity and she was the baby of the family. She said that she rarely had to do any work around the house and that her brothers and sisters did everything for her. Growing up in King's Cross rather than 'down the Hill' meant that she had fewer Italians around her, but that did not stop her from developing a fierce pride in her Italian blood; perhaps it was strengthened. That pride, combined with a fiery temper, meant that she was frequently involved in fights with English or Irish children who she felt were insulting her personally or Italians generally. Despite being only 4 feet 10 inches tall, she was fearless and consequently somewhat feared by the other children in the area. Connie left school at 14 and became apprenticed to a couturier firm in the West End. She loved dressmaking. Throughout her life she returned to it again and again. She worked in the West End throughout the 1930s and during WWII was put to work making uniforms.

The move back to Clerkenwell suited Connie. She loved the bustle of 'The Hill' of the 1930s. She joined in everything from meetings of the Church-run *Figli di Maria* (Children of Mary) to the secular pleasures of dances at the Mazzini-Garibaldi Club. From here she and some of her friends were thrown out one evening because, finding the cloakroom full, they had draped their coats over the bust of Mussolini.

Connie and Carmine

During the war Raffaela was evacuated out of London because of the bombing and her own immobility. She was moved with Annie to Cuffley in Hertfordshire. The rest of the family stayed in London and visited at weekends. Close to Cuffley was a camp for Italian prisoners of war, from which a work party was sent to the village to repair some houses. When they discovered that an old, bedridden Italian lady lived in the village some of the POWs came to visit her. One of these visitors was Carmine Grieco, from Salvitelle in the province of Salerno.

Carmine had been captured in North Africa in January 1941 and was one of the first prisoners to arrive in England, albeit by a circuitous route. After his capture he had been marched to Alexandria in Egypt, where he was put on a ship that had sailed to England via the Suez Canal, Kenya, South Africa and Jamaica! Arriving in Liverpool, he had helped construct a camp on the outskirts of the city. When that was completed, he was moved three or four times to do the same in other parts of the country before being settled in a camp at Newgate Street, Hertfordshire.

Carmine got to know Connie during her visits to Cuffley and gradually an

The Cicco family in 1925

Carmine, Anthony and Connie outside Cavendish Mansions in 1966. 'Clerkenwell Screws', the ironmongers opposite at Nos.107-109 Clerkenwell Road, are still trading today.

understanding developed between them. As the war came to an end, Carmine proposed. Connie's brother Joe, as head of the family, decided that although Carmine seemed a decent sort, he was going to take no chances with his sister's happiness. He wrote to his uncles in Nola and they paid a visit to Salvitelle (no easy task in immediately post-war Italy) to check that Carmine was suitable, with no undisclosed wives or family scandals to upset Connie. They reported back that all was well and Joe gave his blessing.

Carmine was repatriated to Italy while Connie tried to arrange his residency in England. There then followed a long period of form filling and official requests. Thanks to Mr Bennelli (a family friend who owned a café off Regent Street and was willing to act as a sponsor), Carmine arrived in England in 1947. He and Connie were married at the Italian Church in December of that year. Unfortunately Joe had died in the previous June and so it fell to Tony to give Connie away. The relatively recent loss of Joe and the general austerity of the times made the wedding a fairly quiet affair. The reception was held in the flat in Cavendish Mansions, with the bedroom door open so that Raffaela could join in the celebrations from her bed. The wedding proved to be timely, as Raffaela passed away the following February.

Connie and Carmine also got a flat in Cavendish Mansions and in 1950 a son, Antonio (Tony) was born. Carmine tried his hand at a number of jobs in his early years in England including asphalting and making plaster statuettes but he eventually settled in the terrazzo trade. Connie had a number of dressmaking jobs. Connie's three unmarried siblings helped ensure that Tony got a good education but only Mary lived long enough to see it bear fruit.

Phil died in 1961 and Annie in 1969 and Mary stayed close to Connie and her husband and son until her death in 1992. Despite numerous attempts Carmine never managed to persuade Connie that they should move away from Clerkenwell. Connie was too attached to 'The Hill' and all it stood for, and, of course, to the Italian Church, to ever contemplate living anywhere else.

The Church had always played an important part in the life of the Cicco family. From that first day when Salvatore came to the Church in Clerkenwell, he and the family always had the greatest respect for what it stood for and did in the Italian community.

Salvatore often did repair work or made things for the Church. He took his turn carrying the statue of the Madonna during the annual Procession. His wife went to Mass almost every day when the family lived 'down the Hill'. In later life, when her paralysis meant she couldn't get to the Church, one of the priests, usually Padre Crescitelli in the early years (who had been a classmate and friend of Tony), brought her communion every day.

When Carmine married Connie, he too became involved in the life of the Church. He was a member of the Confratelli del Santissimo Sacramento for over 50 years. He first walked in the Procession in 1952, accompanying his 2-year-old son Tony, who was dressed as a Franciscan friar. When a photo of Tony appeared in the *Daily Mail* next morning, the family almost emptied the newsagent's of its stock. Every year thereafter Carmine took part, often carrying the statue of the Madonna as his father-in-law had done in the 1920s. In 2002 he and his son celebrated their 50th anniversary of walking in the Procession. Connie used her dressmaking skills to help in the production of costumes for participants, often taking in or letting out the same costume year after year depending on the size of each year's Pilate or Joseph or Peter.

Connie always had great memories of the processions that took place in the 1920s and 1930s. She remembered how the area around the Church was decorated with garlands across the streets and altars on window ledges festooned with silk hangings and flowers. She particularly enjoyed the bands that played in those days, and the dancing in the streets in the evening after the Procession.

Being naturally gregarious, Connie loved talking to people and hearing their stories. She had a great memory for the various doings of the Little Italy of that time. She was, however, reticent about retelling some of the stories, particularly if they reflected badly on anyone. Her view was that their children and grandchildren were still around and they didn't need to be embarrassed or upset.

As the Italian community of Clerkenwell scattered to all parts of London, Connie stayed. In the 1960s and '70s and even into the '80s, her flat in Cavendish Mansions always seemed to contain someone from 'The Hill', who now lived in Highbury or Finchley or Enfield, and who had popped in for a cup of coffee or tea and a chat about the 'old days'. Even some of the new generation of Italians who arrived after WWII came to Connie's to ask if she would come with them to their children's school, or to the Labour Exchange or the doctor's, to help explain their various problems.

Salvatore's grandchildren

In 2003 Connie and Carmine had to move from Clerkenwell. Old age and illness meant they needed to be closer to their son in Ormskirk, Lancashire. We can't be sure whether Connie realised that she had finally been moved from her beloved Clerkenwell, as dementia had robbed her mind of its previous sharpness. In 2004 Carmine and Connie died within four months of each other. Naturally, they made their last journeys from the Italian Church, past 'The Hill' and up Clerkenwell Road, stopping outside Cavendish Mansions, and eventually passing through Kensal Green Cemetery on their way to meet Salvatore and the rest of the family enjoying their eternal reward.

Almost all the grandchildren of Salvatore and Raffaela have raised families of their own. Cyril and his wife Ida produced two sons and a daughter. Ray and his wife June likewise had two sons and a daughter. Emilio and his wife Pat had two sons. Tony married late in life and he and Caroline have no children. Sadly, Ida and Emilio have died but the next generation flourishes. The children of Cyril, Ray and Emilio have 15 youngsters between them – the real legacy of the man who arrived in the wrong country in 1896.

Rosa Lusardi

written by Olive Besagni after meeting Rosa on holiday

On our first evening an attractive lady looked across the room at my husband Bruno and said "I know you! Didn't you used to live in Victoria Dwellings?" Bruno replied, "Your face looks familiar, but I can't place you." She smiled. "Do you remember the fish shop in Clerkenwell Road?" At this point I butted in. "You're the pretty girl who worked in the fish shop." (I always noticed the girl when I passed Gigatti's; she was so pretty and had an air of refinement about her.)

Her name turned out to be Rosa, and she was quite happy to recall her days as a young girl living with her Auntie in the flat above 'The Holborn Fish Restaurant'. Known to most of 'The Hill' community as 'Gigatti's', this was situated at 160 Clerkenwell Road, opposite Leather Lane, on the fringe of *Il Quartiere Italiano*.

Rosa was born in Italy, where she lived on the family farm in the little village of Chiavenna Rocchetta in the province of Piacenza. She was the eldest daughter among the six children of Ermelina and Luigi Bonomi. She has happy memories of her childhood. She smiled as she recalled the days she spent with her younger brothers and sisters, particularly at the time of year when her father would clean out the big metal bath, then the children's feet would be scrubbed clean, after which the grapes, already collected from the vines, would be laid in the tub. In would go the bare-footed children, jumping up and down on the grapes, crushing them until there was sufficient liquid for the wine making.

One day in the year 1938, Rosa's mother received a letter from her sister Alice, who had emigrated to England and lived in Clerkenwell with her husband Giuseppe Nazzani. She wrote that they were doing very well in London where they were the proprietors of a very busy (fried) fish shop. The couple were childless and Alice asked her sister Ermelina if she would be willing to send their eldest daughter to live with them. She was in a position to give her a good life in a loving home, and ensure that she received a good education, along with the many other material things that her family at home were not in a position to give her. Rosa, who was 13 years old at the time, was naturally excited at the prospect of going to England to stay with her aunt. I'm sure that her mother was reluctant to let her little girl go, but she couldn't stand in the way of her daughter's opportunity for a better life, and at least she would be with family.

So it was that little Rosa Bonomi arrived in London to live with her zia Alice, affectionately known to everyone by the nickname Gigatti. Rosa was enrolled into the Convent in Ely Place, a private school run by nuns. She loved the school and was very proud of her uniform, as you can see in the photograph. She made friends with the children of Famiglia Ricordi, who lived in the flat above theirs over the fish shop. She was unable to communicate with them very well, because so many of the local children were unable to understand Rosa or respond to her in Italian. (The mothers of *Il Quartiere* would address their children in their native dialect, but the children in the main answered in English.) The language barrier was hard for Rosa because her aunt, whilst supplying her with love and attention, would not allow her out to play.

As a result, she was very reserved and shy. A bitter blow for her was the day that she was told by the Sister Superior to bring her aunt to the school. When her aunt arrived there the following morning she was told to remove Rosa at once, as she was no longer welcome in the school, the reason being that Italy had entered the war on the side of the Germans. This meant that Rosa was now an enemy alien and it wouldn't be fair to the other children to allow her to remain in the school. The nun's words clearly hurt the child so much that, as Rosa recounted the incident to me, I could see that the anger was still there.

That was the end of Rosa's school days. She was old enough then to start work, and so automatically helped her *zia* in the fish shop. With her *zio* Giuseppe's death in 1941, her *zia* relied on her company more than ever. The teenage Rosa was happy enough but, looking back, would have liked a little more freedom: although treating her as if she were here own daughter, her aunt was very strict. She would not allow her to go out without her, or without a chaperone. Naturally, through working in the shop, Rosa's English improved and she got on well enough with the customers.

Rosa in school uniform

The week before Rosa's 21st birthday, two young sisters, Maria and Rita Sartori, asked her aunt if she would allow Rosa to go with them to 'The Swiss Club' in Charlotte Street (Fitzrovia). After much pleading on Rosa's part, her aunt finally agreed – provided they brought her home by ten o'clock. Being the pretty girl that she was, she was soon spotted by a young Italian boy, who came over and asked her to dance. She declined, saying that she couldn't dance. He was not to be put off so easily. 'Don't worry', he said, 'I'll teach you'. While they were dancing Rosa mentioned that it was her 21st birthday the following week, that a friend was making a cake and that she was having a few people in to celebrate. The young man ventured, 'Perhaps I could come and have a piece of cake?' Rosa replied, 'I'll have to ask my zia'. She knew that this was not going to be a welcome suggestion, but as she had taken quite a fancy to the young man, she told her zia what he had said. *Zia*, undaunted, said, 'Certainly, he can have a piece of cake, but he's not coming into this house, you can take it outside to him on the doorstep'. In the end Rosa managed to persuade her aunt to let him come in.

There was quite a performance with the cake. As food was still rationed, a young neighbour had said that if Rosa could save enough eggs, she would make the birthday cake. Rosa managed to save six eggs, which she passed on to the neighbour. On her birthday a lovely cake with candles was set out and the Asti was poured. The young man had been allowed to enter and everything was

Rosa and Giovanni on their wedding day in 1947

set. When the time came to cut the cake, it was a catastrophe: they tried all the available knives but no-one was able to penetrate it. In desperation *zia* went down into the shop and got a big knife that was used to cut the fish, and finally the guests were given a hard-won piece of cake. When *zia* Alice was introduced to the young man, she bombarded him with questions, along with the usual "Which part of Italy are you from?" she wanted to know everything, from his wages to his hobbies, and almost asked what his intentions were. It would seem that he passed the test. The young man's name was Giovanni Lusardi; his family originated from Bratto, Pontremoli in the Tuscany region, his income was £3.50 a month, and he worked in a café/restaurant in Dalston. But he never told Rosa or her aunt that his family owned the business until the day of their engagement, when he took her home to meet his family. It seems he too was worried that a girl might marry him for the wrong reasons! However, the couple were married in 1947 and lived happily ever after.

Joe Bacuzzi — 'the Legend'

Joe Bacuzzi was born on 5 October 1916 at No.24 King's Cross Road, a short distance from the Italian Quarter. His mother Natalina Clerici had married Camilli Bacuzzi in Italy. They both originated from Milan or a nearby province. As a rule Italians would give their firstborn son the forename of his father, but in this case they baptised the baby Giuseppe Luigi Davide. This may have been because his father's first name was Camilli, a very unusual name for a man and one for which there appears to be no English translation.

The family moved on, into a flat in a large tenement block, Victoria Dwellings in Farringdon Road, where their neighbours were English families, a couple of German families and a great many Italians. The flats in their particular block were slightly superior to the others, enjoying private indoor toilets and sinks. The young Joe attended St Peter's Italian School in Saffron Hill (later known as Herbal Hill). He was a well-behaved boy and got into very little trouble. The headmaster, Mr Taylor, had a great love of football and the young Bacuzzi's prowess on the pitch was already showing itself. Joe was a hero to his friends. St Peter's Italian School football team, even in those early years, was a force to be reckoned with. Football featured large in the curriculum of St Peter's School; both teachers and boys had a great love for the game. Many cups and trophies were on display in the school hall.

Joe Bacuzzi

When Joe left school he was picked up by the Tufnell Park amateur team, later having trials with Arsenal. Unfortunately he failed to impress the Arsenal hierarchy but in 1935 he was taken up as an amateur by Fulham. At the age of twenty he turned professional and made his first team debut in 1937.

He netted his first goals in the 1938-39 season, when Fulham defeated Luton Town. He made 70 pre-WWII appearances for the side, but in spite of his success, Joe always kept his feet on the ground, and true to his roots, would drink with his old contemporaries in the Coach and Horses pub on Sundays after Mass. He served on the altar at St Peter's Church, as a schoolboy and as a young man. There is no doubt how popular he was with old and young alike, making time to chat and encourage the local youngsters and reminisce with his old friends. Everyone followed his career and they were proud of young Joe – after all, he was from 'Little Italy'.

He made his international debut for England in 1939 against Wales and went on to be capped thirteen times for his country, making his last appearance for England on 19th May 1946 against France. During his international career Joe played with Stanley Matthews, Joe Mercer and Tommy Lawton, who were huge names in the football world.

World War II saw Joe join up to the British Military. In 1943-44 he served in North Africa and Italy. Joe was the Italian hero to all the youngsters 'down the Hill' and was the epitome of every young boy's dream.

After nearly 300 First Team appearances for Fulham, his playing career was finally brought to an end by a knee injury in 1956, after which he became Reserve Team Trainer. Joe continued to live in the Clerkenwell area until his death, aged 78, in 1995.

Charles Nolan's reminiscences

I was born in Farringdon Road within the sound of St Peter's bell ('the dong'). I can therefore claim to be of St Peter's patronage; have been baptised in the church, spending all my schooldays there, making my first Communion there, being confirmed there, and married in the church in 1942.

During all those years I gained many memories of the church, the school, the people and the immediate surroundings. I well remember:

The large timber yard in Back Hill before the Daily Mirror building was built. Miss Mary, Miss Winnie, Miss Lily and Miss Daisy, teachers in the infants' classes. Ringing the school bell regularly in Little Saffron Hill. Playing outside the school as horse-drawn carts delivered to Hunter Penrose [printing equipment suppliers at 109 Farringdon Road]. The Carlo Gatti horse-drawn carts delivering ice in Leicester Place, off Little Saffron Hill, and collecting up fallen pieces to put around milk and butter at home.

The colourful Christmas bazaars which lasted two days in the school hall. Helping Sister Mary make up lucky dips for the bazaar. Taking doorstop sandwiches for morning playtime at school and eating them with milk warmed by teachers around the classroom fire. Putting a bucket of water on the classroom fire to warm, so Miss MacVay could wash her hands at the end of lessons. Collecting the cane and punishment book from Mr Taylor (headmaster). Having your cheek pulled then smacked by shell-shocked Mr Delaney and observing him having a quick pinch of snuff behind the blackboard. Gella's penny corned-beef rolls – you could have them on a Monday, Tuesday, Wednesday, Thursday, Saturday or Sunday – but never on a Friday. Buying a 'ha'penny' of sticky toffee (in newspaper) in Gella's – it could be tiger nuts, jelly babies or a mixture of anything.

Going round classrooms to tell the teachers there would be Benediction during the afternoon (Thursday), walking down the iron stairs, with all the class, into church. Leading the annual outdoor procession – first as a small boy and in later years as a young man swinging the incensory. The church choir being augmented by orchestras and such famous singers as Paolo Silveri. Lighting hundreds of candles on and around the altar, including six large chandeliers hanging from the ceiling during the 40-hour prayers. Seeing the many old Italian ladies entering the church during Holy Week carrying wreaths and boxes of corn for the Altar of Repose. A crowded church, and Father Crescitelli assisting the missionary, standing on a specially constructed dais, draped in black, nailing

Jesus to the Cross during the Good Friday service. Pulling the 'dong' every evening at 7.45pm for Benediction. Receiving chocolates and Easter eggs for altar services at Easter. Coffee and mince pies for the servers, in the school, after Christmas midnight mass. Bottles of lemonade to drink after the outdoor procession, something stronger for the police. Vespers in church every Sunday evening. Procession of the Blessed Sacrament around the church every third Sunday of the month, led by Miss Amelia Malangone and little girls in long white dresses. Fr Kennedy's poignant and moving appeals on behalf of the clergy at Christmas, Easter and Whitsun. Selling programmes in the streets two weeks before the procession. Fr Chiaponcelli striding out, impeccably dressed, in his homburg hat, black gloves and with his shining walking-stick. Christmas parties in our classrooms and parties in the Holborn and Finsbury town halls. Going to the Kingsway Hall for Empire Day Concerts and receiving fresh fruit from the Empire and chocolates as gifts. Travelling on trams to play football with the school at Hackney Marshes. Evacuating the school in an orderly manner for fire drill, and all proceeding to the corner of Saffron Hill for the roll call. Sister Margaret in her ever white, and spotlessly clean, winged head-dress; Sister Angela's black-tasselled shawl and black bag. The many teachers in the 'big boys' classrooms'. Mr Goddard, Mr Murtagh, Mr Stevenson, Miss Leape, Miss Proctor, Mr McKee. Helping Mr Fackler build the crib in church every Christmas. Having to play the part of Edith in *The Private Secretary* at the Central Club, presented by St Peter's Dramatic Club under the direction of Fr Lamb and Bro. James. Mixed dramatic classes (male and female) were not permitted by the church in those days. The piety stall at the top of the church steps – run by the Laurati family. Collecting up almonds and coins from the outside the church after weddings. The endless clatter of Mildner's printing machines [at 140 Clerkenwell Road], heard in the school classroom when the windows were open. Jack Lynsky and Mr White in charge of the boys' club. Mr Balsamo (the barber) whistling up from the pavement to his flat above in Griffin Mansions, when assistance was required in his shop.

Mrs Bruschini collecting for St Anthony's masses. The lamplighter making his way around to light the street gas lamps. Sitting two in a seat during the special children's performances on Saturday mornings at the Globe Cinema on Skinner Street. Signorina Ballestrina, the Italian night school teacher. Tramps calling at the convent for tea and bread. Mr Casey the collector in church. Mr Driscoll, the Master of Ceremonies of the altar servers. Mary Capocci collecting for church flowers. Buying a 'tuppney and pernerf [penn'orth]' in the dripping shop near Laystall Street.

The School's evacuation to Wootton Bassett in 1940. The many outings from the church in Patsy Hearn's coaches. Mr Hearn being 'Godfather' to countless boys (myself included) for confirmation, his sister being 'Godmother' to the girls. The police chasing 'bookmakers' runners' through Warner Street. The statues in Regali's shop near the church. The barrel organs being hired out from the big shop later occupied by Chiappa in Eyre Street Hill. Having woodwork

Charles Nolan's reminiscenses

and metalcraft lessons at Wild Street School, Kingsway. Mr Wheeler being woodwork teacher; Mr Bailey, metalcraft.

Riding past Victoria Dwellings and the Met. [Metropolitan pub] on my ball-bearing skates and my home-made scooter held together by screw-eyes, nuts, bolts, and a 'tarry block' from the road. Driving my home-made wooden cart mounted on four pram wheels, down Back Hill and taking extra care passing the presbytery. Buying my fireworks from Harris the newsagents in Leather Lane. Being taken by my mother to buy my first pair of long trousers (at the age of 13) from Harvey and Thompson in Leather Lane and the tears she shed when I first wore them.

The meeting being called for the 'Hastings boys' at the end classroom of the school – and the lessons we missed. All the 'Hastings boys' leaving Clerkenwell Road by tram (via the Kingsway tunnel) for Charing Cross Station. St Peter's boys walking down the old London Road, Hastings, to attend Sunday mass at 'St Mary's Star of the Sea' in the High Street. Walking in the outdoor procession from the church to Hastings Castle. Mrs Gill, Mr Redfern, Mrs Powell and the other ladies who cared for us in Hastings; Miss Ball at the church there who supervised all the arrangements. Shopping in Hastings for presents to bring home.

At St Peter's, Fathers Anthony, Haines, Hedderman, Gough and Kelly, and many others, having to climb the stairs to the presbytery before the lift was installed. (During WW II the Italian priests were interned, so a group of Irish

Altar boys leading the Italian Procession past Lloyd's tobacco factory in the 1930s

priests came to serve the congregation's needs; in 1953 the church was eventually returned to the guardianship of the Italian priests. – Ed.)

Mrs Faccini scraping the candlesticks in church and cleaning between the pews. Helping Bro. Abel to clean and polish the High Altar, for women were forbidden to walk on the altar in those days. Taking countless chairs from the side altars through the church, and down the iron stairs in to the school hall for concerts – then bringing them all back again after the concert. Collecting funds towards the church Restoration Fund with the aid of cards on which was printed the shape of a crucifix made up of small square boxes, and for every penny collected the donor would prick a hole with a pin in a box. As a young altar serve sitting in the church and listening to countless 'Italian Missions' (see p 53) – yet not understanding a word.

'Down the Hill', Ciccone and Santella's, butchers; Roberto's paper shop with Italian cheroots and cigars; Jones's Dairy; Caliendo's, provisions; Bergamini's, boot repairs; Liriosi's ice cream stalls; Clerini's shop; Mr Capocci in the barbers; Falca's water factory in Baker's Row; the bakers on the corner of Eyre Street Hill and Warner Street.

The class going to Jackman's of Drury Lane to buy our football boots. Mr Henry, who washed the altar servers' cottas and altar linen. Going to the school dentist in Spencer Street, Goswell Road. The acrid and distasteful smells originating from Johnson Matthey's refineries in Leather Lane. Mellow, pleasing aroma of Bondman and Old Holborn tobacco being processed in Lloyd's factory, Clerkenwell Road. The North Hyde Boys Band (from Mill Hill Orphanage) playing 'down the Hill' on the evenings of Friday, Saturday, Sunday and Monday of the processional weekend; and the boys being welcomed into everyone's homes and showered with hospitality from all the neighbourhood.

Father Crescitelli's loud voice rising from the confessional box. Girls skipping 'keep the kettle boiling' with the aid of a very long rope stretched across the width of Saffron Hill. The cat's meat man, a large basket on his arm, going into Victoria Dwellings. Indian toffee man selling his fluffy woolly toffee in pieces of newspaper rolled and shaped into cones. Sunday afternoon as the muffin man, a large tray on his head, and a bell ringing in his hand, walked around the neighbourhood. First day of January 1942, when in soldier's uniform I was married to my wife by Father Chiaponcelli on the high altar. People walking to visit seven neighbouring churches on the annual Maundy Thursday and Good Friday pilgrimage.

I could go on reminiscing, and am sure many readers will join in such nostalgia and be able to enlarge more fully on the events I have mentioned. Though such years are quickly receding into the distant past, their memories, for me, will never fade but remain forever in my thoughts. I am grateful to have lived, played and prayed alongside such friendly and happy people – young and old. The world today could benefit enormously from the example of friendship, harmony, joy and sincerity prevailing in those days in and around the church, the school and 'The Hill'.

Silvio Giovanelli

What a character! I met Silvio through my friend Tina Belli, who worked with him in the Drury Lane coffee shop where he was the manager. Silvio is a truly charismatic character, because he always greets me as 'Dame Olive' – he has such a grand manner that for one electric second I grow two inches taller in the belief that I deserve the title (we can all dream, can't we!).

Silvio's birthplace was Grezzo, a small hamlet outside Bardi. In 1932 his mother Luisa Bracchi married a local boy, Giovanni Giovanelli. The couple's first baby, Giuseppe, was born in Grezzo in 1933, followed by Mario in 1935. During this period, and following in the footsteps of the majority of paesani, Giovanni went off to seek his fortune in England, leaving his wife Luisa and two little sons in Grezzo. Giovanni found work in Clerkenwell in the terrazzo trade, alongside other Italian immigrants, some of them second or even third generation. Giovanni worked hard and was able to return to Grezzo on a couple of occasions to see his wife and sons, though he never managed to save enough money to bring his little family to England. In 1939 Luisa gave birth to a third son, Silvio.

The advent of World War II meant that all hope of the family joining Giovanni in England had to be postponed until the war was over. Giovanni was not to be reunited with his family for eight years. Silvio recalls faint memories of his childhood spent in the mountains. He remembers the retreat of the German army and the arrival of the American and British soldiers.

In 1947, Luisa and her three sons finally arrived in London to join her husband. At last, at the age of eight, Silvio met his father. Their first home was in Whiskin Street, five minutes' walk from *Il Quartiere Italiano*. Silvio attended St Peter's Italian School. Two brothers were born in Britain, Pietro in 1948 and Aldo in 1954. Famiglia Giovanelli was complete. Unfortunately, Luisa's joy was short-lived. Giovanni passed away in 1955, at the age of 55. By this time the three eldest sons were employed, the school leaving age at that time being 14 years.

The young Silvio was employed by 'The Selected Wine Company', a retail wine shop in Great Windmill Street, Soho where he worked from 10am until 3pm, and again from at 5pm to 9pm, extraordinarily long hours for a boy of such tender years. His next place of employment was the well-known Drury Coffee Company where he started in 1970 and worked for many years.

Luisa moved with her boys to Northdown Street, Kings Cross, where they lived for 40 years. The first son to leave the Giovanelli household was Giuseppe,

St Peter's School photo, 1950

Back row L-R: Paul Modica, Terry Cassidy, **Silvio Giovanelli**, Brian Mays, John Weaver, Remo Bruscini, Joseph Oliva, Tony Rossi, Mr McKee

Middle row L-R: Mr Gallantry, Mario Vestuto, Roy Scully, ? McArthur, Peter Ferrari, Terry May, Luigi Rizzi, Remo Scaglioni, David Davighi, Teddy Wood, Tino Frattarol

Front row L-R: James Marcantonio, Razzi Tuffano, Angelo Maestranzi, ? Ascarino, ? D'Agostino, Robert Logli, Vincenzo Boffa, ? Posci, Nino Baccarini, Tony Schiavi, Terry Driscoll, Ray Baccarini

who on 25 October 1959 married Maria Mazzochi. Maria's family came from Bettola in Provincia di Piacenza, northern Italy. Eleven years later, in January 1970, Mario wed Patrizia Balzani, from Florence where the couple now live. Silvio always kept himself busy in and around the Italian community. He was a founder member of St Peter's Boys Club which began in 1960. He spent 22 years on St Peter's Church Committee. He also took part in the Procession for many years. I think we can say that Silvio has done his share in keeping the Italian community spirit going. Although he was never on the committee, he worked alongside Lou Necchi at the well-known Mazzini-Garibaldi Club in Red Lion Street.

The family were shocked when one dreadful day, on 4 April 1977, Luisa, aged 70, was run over by a car in Caledonian Road and fatally injured. Her sons were devastated by her death. The three Giovanelli boys left at home remained bachelors until Silvio married his long-time girlfriend Gemma Rech in 1983. Gemma's family are from Treviso in the Veneto. In June 1991, Aldo married Imelda Edgar in Belfast and the couple now live in Monmouth, South Wales, where many other immigrants from Provincia di Parma settled. Finally, Pietro (Peter) married Sally Steel on 10 October 1992.

In the small village of Grezzo (whence Silvio hailed) there were 29 houses, but today only seven of them are occupied. In 1947 there were apparently 20,000 people living in the Commune di Bardi, but now there are no more than 3,000 left. Nowadays descendants of families who have emigrated across the years return to the land of their fathers at holiday times. In the month of August the returning migrants gather in the Square in Bardi in the evenings and especially on market days. At this time of the year young people, the descendants of new and old emigrants, love to return to their roots, and for the best part of the month the Square in Bardi is swinging; while the older generations meet up with relatives and friends of days gone by.

A great variety of accents may be heard: the English accents with a Welsh lilt of emigrant families from Cacrovoli, mostly in catering; the French ones of those descended from migrants from Baccolo in Tassi, who settled in Paris as chauffage boilermen; and the American accents of immigrants to New York, originally from Gravago.

As August ends, sadness descends on the area and the excitement of the long-awaited holiday in Italia is over. The goodbyes have been said to relatives and to parents who have previously returned to their native land to retire. The Italians are on the move again, this time back to their comfortable homes in whichever country their forebears chose to begin their new lives, and in face of many hardships to make good and gain a better way of life for their families.

Victor Kibble's reminiscences

'The very best of people'

I am hoping that you will enjoy these interesting articles sent to *Backhill* magazine in 1988 by a non-Italian who spent his childhood in the Italian Quarter. Victor lived amongst families like his own, except that the majority of the neighbours were immigrants from another country – Italians who spoke a different language, in a variety of dialects, and had a completely different culture. It must have been very hard living next door to families whose culinary aromas were so different from one's own. While those from the Italians' homes would be of tomatoes, garlic and many and varied herbs, most likely wafting through the air from the Irish abodes would be the smells of cabbage and bacon.

A W Kibble was born in Clerkenwell on 22 March 1923, and attended St Peter's Italian School from 1928 to 1937. He preferred to be called Victor because it felt Italian.

Images from the past: the 1920s

39 Bowling Green Lane, a grand sounding address that conjures up images of a rural paradise, peaceful warm afternoons disturbed only by the gentle clicks of the bowlers' woods as they competed on the green. Number 39 was many worlds apart from such Arcadian dreams – a two-up, two-down drab brick dwelling with a communal lavatory and wash house out in the back yard, set amongst drab buildings that appeared to lean on each other for fear of falling down. Despite their aesthetic shortcomings and the lack of the basic comforts of life, our two small rooms were our world of family love, warmth and affection.

It seemed we could be living in a foreign land, in the surrounding area our neighbours were mostly foreign with a few Irish, the one common factor was the local church where it appeared that almost everyone attended Sunday Mass at St Peter's Italian Church. Once we had settled in our new home we were contented, most of our new neighbours turned out to be Italian immigrants looking for a better life.

I believe that I first became aware of being *'simpatico'* when I lost my heart to a beautiful brown-eyed Italian girl in the infants' at St Peter's. She sat next to me in class and I didn't have the courage to speak to her, but was content to be granted an occasional glance or smile. I spent most of my break times admiring her across a crowded playground.

It broke my heart when the time came to graduate 'upstairs'. I found myself sitting next to another boy who had probably left his heart downstairs as well. We consoled each other by becoming firm friends, even though his command of English was poor and my Italian was confined to 'si' and 'no' accompanied by the appropriate gesture and wave of the hands.

Being a non-Italian, in a minority amongst my school mates, didn't seem strange to me: at that early age I probably thought that all Catholic schools were the same. Our English-speaking teachers appeared to have no problem

St Peter's School football team, 1936-37

communicating with us as a group, except when calling the register, trying to get their tongues around some of the names: Natarro, Nastri, Zecchi, Manzi, Savoni – these were the easy ones. Often a boy could be marked absent, not realising that his name had been called because of a bad pronunciation by the teacher.

To represent St Peter's on the football field was a great achievement, competition for selection was fierce, and to wear the shirt with the green and white badge sewn on the chest was a great honour. I wore mine with pride; 'we Italians' were a match for even the toughest opposition. Although I was an 'adopted Italian' in every sense, my greatest disappointment in those innocent days between the wars was not being eligible to join the 'Young Fascisti'. I envied them in their smart uniforms, parading outside St Peter's after Sunday Mass, marching proudly to the stirring sounds of *Giovinezza*. How naïve we all were in those days!

The Procession of Our Lady of Mount Carmel, was the highlight of our year. On that special day we forgot the drabness of our lives and surroundings, and laughed, sang and danced into the early hours of Monday morning.

The Mortuary

Not one of the most pleasant images of the past. Whoever decided to locate the [Finsbury] borough mortuary in the middle of a highly residential street, Northampton Road, wedged between terraces of two-up and two-down houses, must have had a twisted sense of the macabre. The sombre routine of its activities was there to be witnessed daily by the local residents, adding yet more misery to their already wretched existence, and to the children who played in the road outside.

The rear of the mortuary backed onto 'Swing Gardens' – not much in the way of gardens, but plenty of swings. Only the most daring among us would venture to look in through the back windows, which were left open during the summer months, in an attempt to let in some fresh air for the short term 'residents'. A strong aroma of carbolic disinfectant perpetually hung over Northampton Road and the Swing Gardens [now Spa Fields park]. There was a constant procession of plain horse-drawn vans carrying their gruesome loads in through the narrow, arched entrance gateway, to deposit 'the remains' of some recently departed soul and then depart for their next collection point.

On the long dark winter nights most people would cross to the other side of the road, not daring to pass the mortuary entrance for fear of being dragged over the cobbles into the abyss of darkness beyond by a lonely, ghostly apparition in need of a bit of human companionship.

'Swing Gardens' and Mortuary, Northampton Road

Mrs Neville, the pawnbroker's friend

Five feet tall and distantly related to our family, she apparently had no husband (if he existed I never saw him and he was never spoken about), but she did have a rather odd son called Alfie, pronounced by us as 'Elfie'. Mrs Neville was the local pawnbroker's best and most regular customer. Her bed linen and her "husband's" best suit spent more time on "Uncle's" premises then they did in her own house.

Mrs Neville pledged them every Monday morning and I would redeem them every Saturday morning. I would push the empty battered Victorian bassinette pram down Gray's Inn Road and take my place in the queue of "Saturday redeemers", present the pawn ticket with a half- crown piece, and receive in return three tattered brown-paper parcels tied up with fraying string. Then I would convey Mrs Neville's "precious possessions" back on their long journey home to await their next journey back to "Uncle's" on the following Monday morning.

Victor's own CV

1945: I was now in my 4th year with the Royal Air Force, having survived flying with two operational squadrons. I found myself as an air/ground signals training officer at an airfield 'somewhere' in the Midlands.

1946: Demobbed from the RAF, I made my way back to civvy street to pick up the threads of a career in the fashion trade that had been interrupted by the war. It was a career that was to span 40 years with a multinational fashion organisation.

My job as a senior merchandise buyer entailed worldwide travel, to the Far East and America. One of my major European markets was Italy. There I found that my early links with Italians, through my schooling and the environment I grew up in, opened many doors for me.

1980: I requested an early retirement. This was granted to me in June 1980, but by September 1980 I was finding retirement too tame. I was offered a full-time post as a lecturer at a local college, which I gladly accepted.

1987: Now in my 7th year as a lecturer, but seriously considering a 2nd retirement in order to take up a career in creative writing and illustration.

Since those memorable days I have continued to strengthen my *simpatia* with the Italian people. In the professional career I was a *compratore di moda* and made numerous visits to Italy every year. My holidays were always spent in Italy; the Park Hotel in the village of Cinquale has been my summer retreat for many years. There I was amongst friends, as I was during my happy days at St Peter's.

Lebaldi and his tortoises

The photograph, from a daily newspaper, shows what at first glance looks like a fine lot of potatoes. In fact it depicts a stock of tortoises kept on the roof of Albion Buildings, Back Hill by Beo Lebaldi.

Beo set off to England from Piacenza at some time in the 1880s, making his way on foot through all the countries in between. On arriving, he found his way to *Il Quartiere*, where he became known in later years as '*Bersagliere*' (sharpshooter or marksman). There he married Irene Cavalca and had two children: a son, Oreste, and a daughter, Sylvia. His was one of the first Italian families to live in Albion Buildings.

Beo became involved in the business of selling herbs, seeds, parrots and tortoises from his home and at the local markets, e.g. Leather Lane and Exmouth Street. He was known as a pet shop owner. Keeping his tortoises on the rooftop of Albion Buildings probably did not endear him to his neighbours.

As one of the first importers of birds and tortoises, Beo experienced many problems, mainly because of his lack of knowledge of the animals' natural habitats and their care needs. He was further handicapped by his lack of knowledge of the English language.

Because of these drawbacks he lost many of his imported animals, but he did not give up and continued to make his living this way, though in addition he later started making and selling ice cream around the area to supplement his income.

Peter Bertoncini – a man of many talents

Peter receiving his gold medal

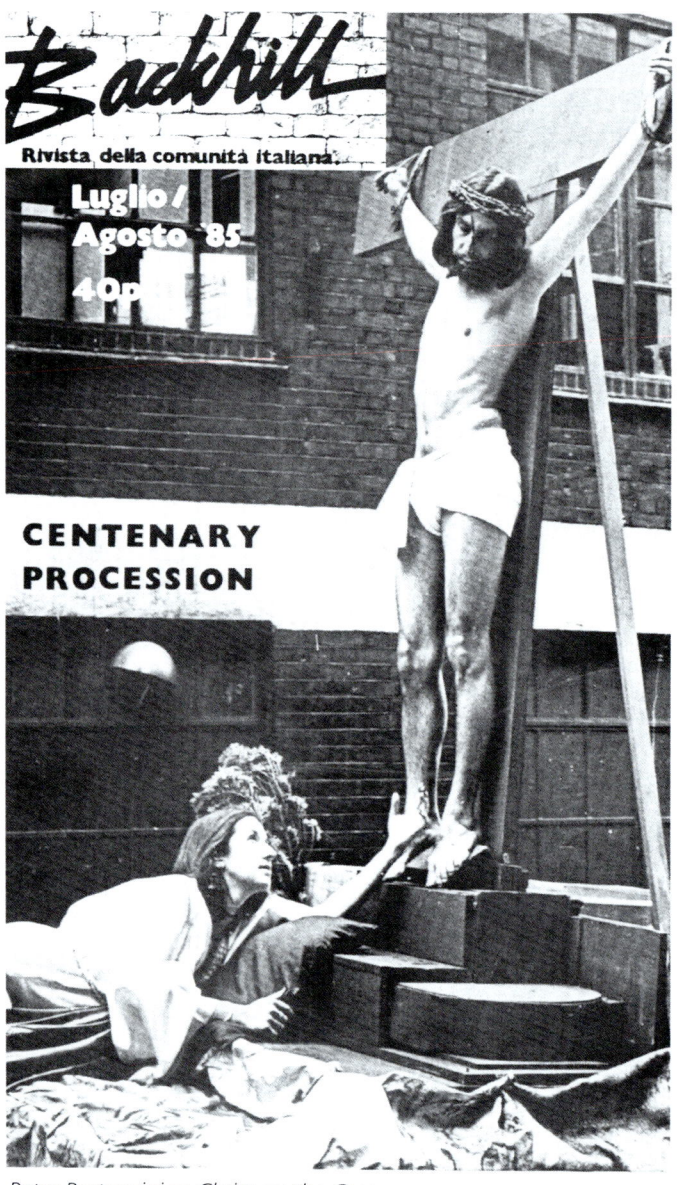

Peter Bertoncini as Christ on the Cross

Peter Bertoncini was born in London on 21 April 1942 of Italian parents, Anna and Giuseppe. He is the eldest of three children.

How can we sum up his very many achievements? With difficulty! He first became active in the community of our church in Clerkenwell when he was 21 years of age. One of his major roles has been in organising the Procession for Our Lady of Mount Carmel from start to finish every July. He started walking in the Procession from the age of five, and as an adult, initially at the request of Father Amoroso, he has ever since been responsible for designing and building floats, and designing and making many of the costumes, with the help of the women's associations such as the Children of Mary. He has always been the leader of a group of men who, two weeks before the big day, begin painting and preparing most of the floats in the basement of the Priests' House on Back Hill and then, on the Saturday morning, assembling them outside in the street.

For many years Peter played the role of Jesus on the Cross. On one unforgettable occasion, as the floats drove sedately along Warner Street, the top of the cross became stuck under the Rosebery Avenue bridge. Everyone gasped – what was to be done? The ever resourceful Peter got a message through to his good friend Modesto, who raced back to the Priests' House and reappeared almost immediately with a saw, which he handed up to Peter, waiting desperately on his float. Having rectified the problem, Peter then clambered back up onto his cross as before and the Procession was able to continue. (There is no mention of this in the Gospels.)

Another of Peter's major tasks over many years has been to decorate the church with flowers. Everyone entering the church on a special occasion is overwhelmed by the beauty of Peter's artistic arrangements. He displays his artistic talents in so many ways, of which the following are but a few. For a number of years he had an Italian drama group called the Arlecchino Players, with whom he produced a number of plays, notably *The Life of Verdi*, written with Giovanna Giacon, and Eduardo De Filippo's *Saturday, Sunday, Monday*. Italian cooking is another of his skills and he has done the catering for many good causes such as church events. Peter is also a first-rate dressmaker and tailor, and has designed and made wedding dresses for many brides in the Italian community. He will even attend the wedding ceremony and the following celebrations to ensure that everything runs smoothly.

Another example of Peter's wide-ranging skills is the life-sized crib or nativity scene which he creates each Christmas in St Peter's Italian Church. It normally takes him two whole weeks to complete the scene. At Easter he produces an amazing Passion play enacted by members of the church. In addition to all this, he is a wonderful friend to many and would never refuse a favour to anyone. He is indeed a true Christian.

On 12 September 1993 Peter received a well-deserved honour from the Provincia di Lucca, whence his family had originated. At a ceremony in the Chamber of Commerce in Lucca he was presented with la medaglia d'oro, bestowed on him as '*un lucchese che ha onorato Lucca ned mondo*'.

Mario Fabrizi — the comic actor

Mario Fabrizi was born in Holborn, to Italian parents, on 1 January 1924. His mother's maiden name was Pisani and his father was a 'viscount' (visconte). Mario was to inherit his father's title after the latter's death in 1959. In his early years he attended St Peter's Italian School.

He became involved in show business and quickly achieved his ambition of becoming well known as an actor and comedian; with his luxuriant moustache, he became a familiar and well-loved face in both film and television. Early in his career he became famous for his 22 appearances in *Hancock's Half Hour*, on both radio and TV, and in Hancock films such as *The Rebel* and particularly *The Punch and Judy Man* in which he played a major role and gained critical acclaim. He was also well loved as Lance Corporal 'Moosh' Merryweather in ITV's 1950s sitcom *The Army Game*.

Over 20 years Mario appeared in many films, notably with Peter Sellers and Spike Milligan. Among the best known are *Two Way Stretch* (1960), *Carry on Cruising* (1962), *The Wrong Arm of the Law* (1963) and *The Pink Panther* (1963).

On 28 May 1960 he married Katherine Boyne, a beautician from Leeds. A son, Anthony, was born the following year and grew up to be a businessman.

The marriage was to last only three years, as on 5 April 1963 Mario died unexpectedly at the family home in Neasden from a stress-related heart attack. As is so often the case with actors, he had been 'resting' for over four months, and only two weeks before his untimely death had announced that he was 'fed up' with having no work and was intending to give up the acting profession. He was laid to rest in St Mary's Roman Catholic Cemetery in Kensal Green.

The Mazzini-Garibaldi Club

Mazzini and Garibaldi – who were they? Giuseppe Garibaldi was born in Nice in 1807. Giuseppe Mazzini was a politician and journalist, born in Genoa in 1805. He was exiled to London, first in 1837, for organising revolutionary uprisings against the authorities at that time in various parts of Italy. He was a hero to Italian youth and later, with Garibaldi, formed the secret society La Giovane Italia (Young Italy) to fight for Italian unification.

Giuseppe Mazzini

In 1864, again in London, he met General Garibaldi who, on a visit to England, was acclaimed by all the Italians in London as a great hero. As a soldier, he had by then famously fought a number of battles to bring about the unification of Italy as a single state. Both men had a high regard for the Italian working man and the ordinary soldier, and great concern for their welfare. For this reason, and during Garibaldi's visit, they founded a club called *Agli Operai Italiani in Londra* (Italian Operatives' Society in London), whose first premises were above a shop at No.64 Farringdon Road, Clerkenwell. Mazzini was invited to be its first president. It was subsequently housed above Di Guiseppe's barber's

Giuseppe Garibaldi

shop in Laystall Street, where there is still a commemorative plaque. In 1933 the club moved to much more spacious premises at No. 51 Red Lion Street, Holborn. On the ground floor was a large bar, on the first floor a spacious banqueting room with a second bar, on the second floor a meeting room and kitchen, and above that a small flat where the steward lived. When Italy entered the Second World War, initially on the side of the Germans, the club closed because the majority of members had been interned, and the British government commandeered the building.

After the war a committee was formed to reopen the club and each member contributed £25 towards the cost. The first post-war president was Serafino Pini, followed in later years by Lino Quaradagini and Gino Bastiani. The club was a big success. Membership grew and it became one of the most popular venues where Italians could meet other Italians – and where boys could meet girls, and girls boys! One important source of income was letting a room in the building on a weekly basis to two Freemasons' lodges, the Lodge Italia and an English lodge.

At Easter the club would lay on *Bacala* (a dried salted cod) served with *Polenta* (a maize flour.) I remember going to the club on a Good Friday and seeing what appeared to be a men-only dinner. The men were all tucking in, and I never did find out why there were only males at that Good Friday feast.

One of the many outstanding occasions arranged for club members was the annual dinner and dance held on New Year's Eve, usually at the Café Royal in Regent Street, in London's West End. This was the headquarters of Lord Charles Forte, himself an immigrant from Italy. Oh, how the members enjoyed themselves! Dressing up was the order of the day; almost without exception the ladies wore beautiful evening dresses and the men wore black ties. There was always a tombola with lavish prizes, the top prize often being two plane tickets for a holiday in Italy.

On another occasion there was great excitement in the club, particularly amongst male members, when it was announced that there would be a visit by the world-famous film stars Gianna Maria Canale and Gina Lollobrigida, who were in London to promote their latest film.

As part of the club's Christmas programme there was always a very popular

The M-G Club befana in 1985

children's party (*befana*). Father Christmas attended, with really lovely presents for all the children, who were also entertained with children's cine films and lots of party food. Mamas and Papas were excluded from the party and had to wait downstairs, where at least they could enjoy a glass of vino.

For many years, my husband Bruno Besagni organised the club's football team, ran the bar and maintained the fabric of the building; he now looks back fondly on his years devoted to the club. Sadly, as with so many clubs, owing to increasingly draconian drink-drive laws and changing tastes among younger people, and because many Italian families had moved away from the area, membership eventually declined and the club finally closed in 2008.

The building was sold and the proceeds from the sale are now held and administered by a charity, the newly formed Mazzini Garibaldi Foundation.

The annual *Scampagnata*

Club members and friends always looked forward to the Italian *Scampagnata* – the picnic to end all picnics. It took place at many different venues over the years; among the most popular was 'Suttons', at Hornchurch, Essex. On one particular occasion we set off in the pouring rain to another venue, near Sutton in Surrey, inaptly named 'Little California'.

In the early days four or five coaches waited outside the Mazzini-Garibaldi Club. The ensuing racket as the participants boarded the coaches had to be heard to be believed – Mama calling to her children: "Vieni, vieni, 'urry up, get on, get on, we're going soon!" As the coach revved up, the singing started, as usual on any such occasion with *Quel Mazzolin di Fiori, que vien de la montagna* – 'that bouquet of flowers which comes from the mountain' – the most popular song at any gathering of Italians. Within minutes the wine would be flowing, and biscotti handed out to everyone within reach, and dolci to the children.

In later years, more and more people decided to come by car, which meant that some of the conviviality on the coaches was lost. Eventually there would be only one, or perhaps two, coaches, and those who came by car, often the younger ones, could come and go as they pleased, although most of them stayed to the end.

On arrival at the ground, everyone claimed their territory and spread out a sumptuous feast on a blanket or on a picnic table with white cloth and napkins, and even once a candelabra! Across the field wafted the scent of oil, vinegar, salami and mortadella, on some tables was champagne in an ice-bucket, and everywhere were traditional bottles of chianti in their unmistakeable wicker flasks. There were children running everywhere, from table to table, picking up titbits as they went, trying everyone's potato or spinach torta . The club committee erected a marquee where they would set up a bar and an ice cream stall, particularly popular when it rained. In addition, Mass was held in the marquee around midday, always very well attended. The Italian atmosphere was enhanced by the sound of Italian songs played over the loudspeakers.

There were always traditional sports: running, egg & spoon, three-legged and sack races. There was strong competition among the men and the mothers; I remember Rita Capella flying down the field, always winning her age group (I was so jealous!) The sports were very well organised and of course the teenagers loved it. My own daughter always won her races (but then she was head of PE at La Sainte Union Convent, Highgate Road).

The Scampagnata, Little California, 1955

The annual picnic in 1966-67

Pieces by Achille Pompa

Achille Pompa, who served as Secretary of the London Ice Cream Association, submitted a number of fascinating and informative articles to *Backhill* magazine. Here are three examples and an edited version of a fourth:

'Little Italy's lost art and artistes'

This is the story of Madame Stauder, who made surgical corsets for hospital patients, and of one of her many Italian girls who helped to make them. She believed in advertising and took large spaces in magazines, etc. She was quite a celebrity. Her husband was a retired Lutheran minister who spent the day fully dressed for a stroll (which he never took!) stretched out on a chaise longue, drinking black coffee and reading newspapers.

Achille Pompa

One of the girls employed there was Teresa Perella. Her father was the famous *"Bersagliere"* (his old regiment in Italy) who became the local 'Ice King,' with many horses and carts serving customers all over London. He even took on the 'Block Ice King,' Carlo Gatti's Pure Ice Company, etc. and brought down their price per cwt [hundredweight] of block ice.

Teresa was a born artist, mimic, singer, comedienne and actress, with an astonishing memory and plenty of *joie de vivre*. One day she astonished everyone by going through the whole of the soprano parts of Mascagni's *Cavalleria Rusticana*, thrilling the two Stauders who were great music lovers, and the other ten girls in the busy workroom.

Teresa married Carmine Ciccone whose father owned the butcher's shop in Eyre Street Hill. Teresa opened her own café opposite King's Cross Police Station. After the Second World War the family opened a small café in Long Lane, Smithfield. Her two middle sons branched out on their own and proceeded to open snack bars in the City of London.

Her mother, Santuccia, was one of the first of many to come from Picinisco, near Cassino and take up ice cream making and selling, creating a vast industry without being conscious of doing so. She never saw her pretty village again after she had left it with her soldier bridegroom. He always looked smart with the

An ice house in Little Italy

traditional black feathers in his large round flat hat and was as athletic as any of his mates in the famous *Bersagliere* March, the fastest in the world (66 steps to the minute, all slanting forward, not upright.)

Teresa had a remarkable ability to compose satirical poems at the drop of a hat on political or any other subjects, leaving the audience doubled up with laughter. One of them, on the delights and drawbacks of dear old Picinisco, was actually duplicated and passed around left and right. What a charming character she was, unique in that pandemonium of many years ago in "Little Italy" at which the Italians of Soho sneered, referring to it as Abyssinia, the End of the World, etc. There was poverty, hard work, ill treatment of young employees, but none of the vices of Soho!

'Steamboat Serenade'

At *La Bella Venezia* restaurant, in Great Bath Street (what remains of which is now Topham Street), lived Alessandro Valente, a singer who later made an album of *Pagliacci* for HMV. Not far away, a famous artists' model, Di Troia, had a niece called Miranda Palma Marcantoni, from the well-known Brighton ice cream family. It coincided that both artists were free for the London Ice Cream Association's outing to Hampton Court and entertained some 250 music lover lovers with operatic arias, Neapolitan songs, etc. It was sheer delight, really a day never to be forgotten.

But there was even better to follow. As the steamer chugged its way back to Westminster it got darker and darker, and London had one of the most beautiful sunsets ever seen. The following morning most newspapers referred to "the magic of the sky." Later even some magazines joined the chorus! The sky became blue, dark blue and turquoise, indigo. Great big stars illuminated the sky, even Jupiter and Venus shone like two suns in that heaven of all heavens, and the singing went on and on. Alessandro and Miranda never seemed to get tired. They asked for no fee but had all the champagne they wanted, to lubricate their throats.

Steamers passing us on their way to Richmond, Twickenham and Hampton Court slowed down and their passengers joined in the never-ending applause. One or two of the steamers even went backwards as a special treat for their customers. And what a treat! A real one, talked about for days and days to follow. No other evening and night have ever equalled it: never!

'Buckingham Palace'

Queen Victoria was a great lover of Italy and all things Italian. In about 1900 six Italian travelling musicians from Clerkenwell's "Little Italy" were invited somehow or other to play for the Queen in Buckingham Palace. One was *Cimmarugheglio*, Antonio Mancini, who played the *cimmaruga;* another was, less certainly, Antonio Perella, known as *Bersagliere* from his Italian Army days. They were "washed and dressed" and played tune after tune in a room near an open door where sat the Queen and her ladies-in-waiting. A majordomo (hereafter addressed as *Eccellenza*) handed them two gold sovereigns and said the Queen was very pleased indeed, and thanked them.

Were they pleased? Yes, to a certain extent. Yet, here was a chance in a million to pay off an old score with the police. They complained that the police always shifted them here and there, making it impossible for them to earn any money. *Eccellenza* said: "Leave it to me – I'll do my best," and disappeared for several minutes. He returned with an official letter saying that Her Majesty was interested in these poor musicians far away from their families, blue sky, lovely country, etc. etc., and hoped that the police would allow them some means of earning a living. Thanks – and so back to Clerkenwell, where copies of the letter were made and distributed around other *compagnie*, i.e. groups of players, all over the country. How the police hated having those letters waved under their noses when they tried to shift the men!

'St Peter's Italian Church'

St Peter's is an exact replica of San Crisogono in Trastevere, Rome, which has always been run by the Pallotini Fathers. It was opened by our first cardinal, Cardinal Wiseman, on 16th April, 1863 before a most distinguished gathering, including the Irish architect, Mr John Miller-Bryson. The church originally held

Pioeces by Achille Pompa

St Peter's Italian Church: exterior and interior

2,000 people; it now holds 3,500 and the crypt 300. There were three entrances: in George Yard off Hatton Wall (swept away in the construction of Clerkenwell Road), Back Hill on the left where the presbytery is, and Little Saffron Hill on the right which was to have been the monumental entrance now situated on Clerkenwell Road, where it was installed in 1878. The bell with its Italian tone, made by Vickers & Sons, weighs four tons and was exhibited at the International Exhibition of 1862.

The beautiful paintings, now replaced, were by Arnaud of Caraglia and Cavaliere Gauthier of Saluzzo. The work took ten months in 1885-6 and the church was reopened on 16th May 1886 by Rt Rev. W.L. Patterson, Bishop of Emmaus. It was described as "the most highly decorated church in England", highly praised, like the Jesuits' Church in Rome, with all its gold.

Italian kings, queens, ministers, and famous singers (Caruso, Gigli) have been regular visitors. The organ with its wonderful sound ensured that all services were packed with people. It is now the parish church for all Italians in London by way of a special decree. Here they can be baptised confirmed, married and have requiem masses said for them. On Sundays Italians come from all over for the masses and the special sermons given by visiting priests from Italy.

Mention should be made of the truly magnificent Roman mosaic of the Twelve Apostles which can be found across the top of the church entrance. One of the heads on the extreme right was damaged by a blast during World War I. It could have been painted over skilfully, but unfortunately it wasn't. Instead the twelve glories were sadly chipped away, and without consultation or advice were replaced by paintings, just as the original Italian paintings by Arnaud and Gauthier were replaced inside the church in 1885.

Angelo Carlo Dainesi — legitimate son of his own craft

An article from the London Italian newspaper *Londra – Roma*, 16 March 1909, submitted to Backhill magazine by Giovanna Servini

Anyone who, walking along Clerkenwell Road towards Farringdon Road, arrives on the corner of Back Hill, will notice on their left, protruding above the pavement from the first floor, a flamboyant sign in the shape of a record, on which are described the principal industries of the adjoining workshop – that of our brilliant fellow countryman Sig. Angelo Carlo Dainese, whose name is so popular in "Little Italy."

Contrary to its more than modest outward appearance, this workshop is nevertheless a veritable encyclopaedia of hand-made products – there are the most exquisite articles in gold coloured metal, candlesticks, hooks, chandeliers, all manner of beautiful ornaments; flowers and a vast collection of showpieces; sculptured works in iron, copper, brass and bronze, that immediately catch the eye with their originality, beauty, elegance and style; in one word, a veritable museum of ingenuity. All this has won for this brilliant artist seven diplomas and three medals at the recent International Exhibition and yet another diploma and silver medal at the most recent Italian exhibition in London.

Worthy son of his art, Signor Dainesi is the Englishman's "self-made man". Given to the art of the smithy from the tender age of ten, and not wishing to be a burden to his widowed mother, he attended industrial and professional evening classes for technical experience. At 15 he became a member of the *Societa Archimede* of the blacksmith mechanics and metal workers of Milan.

Aged seventeen he became self-employed and founded a mechanic's business, inventing new devices, thus preparing himself for the National Exhibition of Milan in 1881, where he won four distinctive honours. When the time came for him to do his military service, he brought his brothers, Gaetano and Ernesto, into the business as partners. Once enrolled as a soldier he asked to be sent to the *Arsenale Militare di Piacenz* where he was one of the first in the mechanics' exams, and was promoted to the *Prima Compagnia Operai D'artiglieria da Costa del 14th Reggimento da Fortezza*, stationed in Genoa. It was at the *Cirie Camp* that he was promoted to lance-corporal and sent to La Spezia. Once discharged from the army he returned to Milan, where he and his brothers decided to sell the business and realise his dream of travelling abroad, as soon as possible.

In the meantime he invented a new sight for guns and cannons that avoided a deviation in the line of fire. Patented in many countries, this invention was successfully tried and approved at the shooting camp in Wimbledon, as was reported in the "Times" and many other European publications, and in several

Belgian periodicals, and it was for Belgium that the patent was bought by the great arms manufacturer, M. Auguste Francotte of Liège.

In 1889 he took the bronze medal and the diploma of honour at the International Exhibition of Agricultural Machinery at Padua and Lodi; and having invented the new, very useful floating indicator for steam boilers, and obtaining the patent for this in Italy, and having learned English in his free time, he came to this country and worked as a mechanic in many French, American and English firms and became a member of the Amalgamated Society of Engineers. Diligent and studious frequenter of the Patent Office Library and Reading Room of the British Museum (pride of our own Antonio Panizzi) as he was, A.C. Dainesi was awarded yet three more patents for as many useful and ingenious inventions by the British government, and in 1895 founded the above-mentioned firm, which he expanded within the space of a few years, adding new departments for trading in furniture and upholstery. He built up a clientele, not only from our own fellow countrymen, but amongst the more exclusive English industrialists, the most illustrious of whom [were] none other than Barker and Co., coach-makers by appointment to His Majesty King Edward VII.

St Peter's RC Boys' School, Class V in 1935; Bruno Besagni is in the 2nd row, 2nd from the left. (see p 45)

St Peter's Italian School, 1931-1940

**Excerpts from the Headmaster's diary –
salvaged from the ruins of the school,
which suffered bomb damage during World War II,
and submitted by Bruno Besagni**

[Undated]: A number of children are attending a pantomime at the Working Mens' Club [the Central Club, Clerkenwell Road].

17.6.1931: Class 1 went by river to Kew Gardens on an educational visit accompanied by Mr Delaney and myself.

22.7.1931: I am retiring on this date. J. Taylor.

25.8.1931: I commenced duty as Headmaster here on this date. J. McKee.

31.8.1931: Mr F.V. Murtagh was given permission to inflict 'slight corporal punishment'.

2.10.1932: Examination by Canon Sutcliffe and Mgr Daly and Father Murphy. 9 certificates and 7 medals awarded. Report read: This school as usual gained the general mark 'excellent', the boys were well advanced for their age. The answering generally was very satisfactory. Division D was not quite up to the standard of the other classes but even it had answered very well. Church music was sung very well indeed and the prayers were said reverently and with hardly a mistake.

18.1.1933: Diocesan examination by Frs Murphy and Darbey. Two superior certificates of merit, 13 certificates of merit and 7 medals awarded.

1.3.1933: District inspector, Mr Pegrin, called regarding numbers for year 1933-34. My estimate to him (Dec. 1932) was for 310 children on books after Easter 1933. Several children, apart from average scholars, have since left and the estimate is now 300, which will not justify an additional assistant as requested.

29.1.1934: This school is again classed 'very good,' as it approached the mark 'excellent'. The answering was generally very satisfactory, but Division F and G, though knowing the words of the Catechism very well indeed, were not so good in doctrine. Religious music was sung very well on the whole, but Division E rendered the Credo only partly well. The prayers were said reverently and with hardly a mistake.

4.7.1934: The 'Potted Sports' Competition, open to all London elementary schools, was won, and the trophy, a replica of a large crow in brass, is held for one year.

31.10.1934: The reason for having a 'floating staff' supply teacher is because of the language difficulty, not numbers.

27.8.1935: The school did not reopen today as it would normally have done at the conclusion of the summer vacation because the interior painting and decorating was not completed. I attended to all outstanding correspondence today.

2.9.1935: The school reopened today after the summer holidays – mainly due to stopping, visiting Italy, and extended holidays.

11.10.1935: Class 3, consisting whose average age is about eleven and three-quarters, charges of Mr Stevenson, spent today at Hackney Marsh Open Air School. The class will spend the whole of every Friday throughout the year there, and as much time as possible has to be spent in taking the lessons in the open air. A charabanc takes the children to and from Hackney Marsh leaving here at 10am and arriving back at 4.30pm.

2.3.1936: Diocesan Examination: we should like to see a crucifix in every room of the school and in a prominent position, and a shrine of our lady would be of the greatest assistance to the devotion of the children, if there were a small one in each class. Nothing can take the place of these aids to the devotion. The school on the whole has reached a high standard and is classed 'excellent'.

2.4.1936: I regret to have to record today the death in school of Joseph Paulini. He collapsed during play at 3.24pm and died in my room within a few minutes. Body taken to the mortuary at Royal Free Hospital.

3.4.1936: Coroner's Office called and informed me that the boy had been found to have a congenital disease of the heart and was liable to die at any time: no inquest.

23.11.1936: Received notification that we can make use of the new open space at Spa Fields, Finsbury, for organised games on Tuesday afternoons.

4.5.1937: Visit of the Deputy Mayor of Holborn, Ald. Langdon, with his wife and two Holborn Councillors, to distribute Holborn Borough Coronation Souvenirs. 10am.

Class II, 1937

12.5.1937: Boys in the charge of Mr Goddard were part of a contingent of 37,000 London schoolchildren lining the Embankment on the occasion of the Coronation of King George VI and Queen Elizabeth.

28.5.1937: Every boy spent a day at Hadley Woods at the invitation of Holborn Borough Council's Coronation celebrations.

17.6.1937: 150 boys were entertained at Gray's Inn. It was a coronation celebration.

26.1.1939: 190 boys were prepared to go away with the teachers if it were found necessary to evacuate them. All the staff were accompanying them. We had to be prepared to get to Holborn Tube Station at a moment's notice. From thence I believe we had Ealing as our railhead. Everybody was pleased when the necessity did not arise and a special holiday was given by the LCC on 7th October in recognition of the splendid behaviour of the teachers and children under the strain of the crisis.

20.5.1939: Final detailed instructions from the Director, Dispersals Officer *re* evacuation received. Mr F.V. Murtagh and I are attending a 12 sessions course in first aid at Kingsway Institute.

1.9.1939: evacuation carried out [to Wootton Bassett, Wiltshire.]

11.3.1940: St Peter's Italian Emergency school opened. Head: J. McKee; Assistants: Sister Agnes; Miss Widmer; Mr Murtagh.

Children evacuated from St Peter's School during World War II; Father Thomas and Sister Patricia; among the children, Cooper (twins), Cicco, Sartori, Maria Falconi, Antonietta & Maria Antonioni, Angela Gargiulo, Johnny Sossi, Alma Antonioni, Doloris Gargiulo, Maria & Lidia Casali, and Vincent Falconi (photo and names submitted by Maria Antonioni of Frewell House, Bourne Estate)

Miranda Sedgwick (née Franchi)
'Memories of my childhood', recorded in 1984

The person who has had the most influence on my life was my *Nonna*, Mrs T Notaro from No.37 Eyre Street Hill. She came to London at a very early age because she had been orphaned. She met my grandfather whom we all called *Papa Nonno* and married him before she was twenty years old. They had many children but only eight survived. They all went to St Peter's Italian School. *Nonna* and *Papa Nonno* worked hard and eventually ran their own business (a café) in Eyre Street Hill. Their children all married children of other Italians and so the café always had lots of family gatherings. It was a place of love and warmth.

I am third generation and, together with my 15 cousins, attended St Peter's Italian School. My teacher, Sister Agnes, had at some stage taught my mother! Every day we would go from school to *Nonna's* and have lunch. This consisted of lovely steaming hot soups, spaghetti and many other mouth-watering delicacies. She was a wonderful cook.

Nonna and *Papa Nonno* were never idle. They made their own ice cream, wine, cheeses and some of my earliest memories are of being allowed to tread the grapes, stir the ice cream, and dip my bread in the wine.

My *Nonna* was a tall, kindly-faced person. She always had a smile. She also never mastered English properly and many were the times the Post Office staff and local shopkeepers tried and failed to understand what she was saying. When she died at age 83 years, although she had been here 60 years, she could not speak anything but pidgin English.

One of the highlights of our young lives was when *Nonna* and *Papa Nonno* had a disagreement – wow! - that was excitement! Voices were raised, arms were in the air and the wrongdoing was fully discussed over and over. We always knew, though, that it would soon be settled, they loved each other so much.

Christmas Eve after Midnight Mass was a magic time. *Nonna* used to prepare a celebration meal for just her family – candles would be alight everywhere, Italian music would be played and *Nonna* used to dance a *Tarantella*. She danced round and round; *Papa Nonno* looked so proud – it was a beautiful sight.

On the Feast of our Lady of Mount Carmel *Nonna* used to adorn their part of 'The Hill' with lots of decorations. Across the street she used to hang balls of flowers and inside the balls were white doves. When *Nonna's* favourite saints, St Lucy and St Anthony, were carried under the decorations, she pulled ribbons, the balls would open, and doves would flutter round the heads of the statues. We grandchildren walked in the Procession and after Mass we used to hurry down to *Nonna's* for some food, pizza and wine and enormous peaches. Someone played the accordion and dancing in the streets was the order of the day. We generally had some item of new clothing for Procession Sunday and *Nonna* was the first person you wanted to show. She made you feel so good: '*che bella!*' she used to say. If you were ill, *Nonna* always had some cure: she had time for everyone.

She used to take us to the old picture house, The Globe, and what a treat it was! She would prepare food as if you were going for the day instead of a couple of hours, and all through the film her hand would keep coming out with lots of goodies. On our return home she would let us go to Manze's in Exmouth Street [Market] and watch the jellied eels being chopped up. Bliss!

Nonna has been dead now for many years and yet there is never a time in our conversation when she is not mentioned. I think of her every single day and remember with such clarity the many petticoats she wore, her comfortable slippers and her funny glasses. Most of all I remember my wonderful happy childhood.

Miranda Sedgwick (née Franchi)

Mamie Secchi

Marie Louise Secchi, always known as Mamie, was born in New York on 23 October 1894. Her maiden name was De Marco. She came to England with her family in 1900 when her father, who ran a terrazzo business, was accidentally killed on a building site.

She lived with her mother, sister Natalie and brother Ernie in Great Bath Street, and went to St Peter's School, Clerkenwell. Her great friends were Bessie Santini, Carmela Monte and Mary Zanelli. She left school at 14 and went to work in Comoy's tobacco pipe factory in Rosebery Avenue, and attended evening classes to learn Italian and French.

At the age of 21, in 1916, she married Frank Secchi at St Peter's Italian Church, and their first home was in Yardley Street, off Rosebery Avenue. She had two sons, Ernest, born in 1921, and Anthony, born in 1932. The family later moved to Wilmington Square and both boys attended St Peter's School. She always used local shops, Bessie Santini's shop, called 'Mariani's' (and later 'Gazzano's'), and 'Terroni's', and remembered well the office in the corner of the shop where newly arrived Italians were helped to interpret their English papers and official documents. She also remembered Rhesteghini's Coach & Horses public house, whose landlord Lou was a great friend of her husband Frank – the pair were known as *Brutto e Bello*. Another of her memories was having the Sunday joint cooked in the local baker's for two old pence. The dancing bears which performed at weekends in Back Hill also remained strongly in her memory. She frequented Exmouth Street market where she knew all the shopkeepers and stallholders and was equally well known to them.

At the outbreak of World War II in 1939 the older son Ernie joined the army and the younger, Tony, was evacuated with his school to Wootton Bassett near Swindon. Unfortunately Tony broke his leg in 1940 and came home, only for the family to be bombed out twice in three weeks. They finally took up residence in Great Percy Street, now attending the church and school of St Peter and St Paul in Amwell Street.

Mamie worked in the Vidor Battery Factory in Gray's Inn Road for the duration of the war. She spent the remainder of her working life in 'The Vintage House' in Old Compton Street, Soho. After the war she visited New York on two occasions to see her family and particularly her mother, who was 102 when she died.

Mamie's elder son Ernie married in 1955 and lived in Wharton Street, just off Lloyd Square. Her husband Frank died in an industrial accident in 1962. She spent her final years living with her younger son Tony. In the late 1970's they moved to a ground floor flat in 'The Triangle', Goswell Road, where Mamie was very happy. Unfortunately she sustained two falls shortly after moving and this restricted her movements out of doors, and her general health and mobility deteriorated so that finally she was confined to a wheelchair. Despite her many ailments her mind remained as sharp as a tack and she was a happy and cheerful person with a great sense of humour. She thrived on company and loved people.

Sadly she lost her elder son Ernie to a heart attack. The final blow, in November 1987, was the terrible fire disaster at King's Cross Underground Station, in which she lost her favourite niece Natalie Falco, a beautiful young woman loved by everyone. Mamie was devastated.

These blows obviously took their toll but she never lost her tolerance, patience and her great faith in God, despite her many infirmities. She loved going out to restaurants, shops, parties and visiting parks. She was optimistic to the end; after her final visit to Bart's Hospital, one of her last observations was: 'I may not be able to run a marathon but at least I will be able to get about on my own'

A coach outing from the Coach & Horses

The Fratellanza Club fracas

Darby Sabini, photographed in the late 1940s

The Fratellanza Club on the corner of Warner Street and Great Bath Street was the only private drinking club of any size actually within the confines of 'The Hill' itself, and so conveniently placed for the local residents.

The club came to national attention in 1922. There had been a history of animosity between two families and the gangs surrounding them, the Cortesis and the Sabinis. Both families were fighting for control of bookmakers' pitches at racecourses around the country, and both gangs frequented the Fratellanza Club at that time.

Late in the evening of 20 November the club owner's daughter and barmaid, Louisa Doralli, was preparing to close up for the night when in burst two Cortesi brothers, Augustus (Gus) and Enrico, with other members of their gang, clearly looking for trouble and for a fight with the Sabinis. Darby Sabini and his younger brother Harry (Harryboy) were in the club at the time. Gus Cortesi pulled out a revolver and was about to fire a shot at Harry Sabini when Louisa jumped from the bar and deflected his arm and the shot missed its target.

Realising that his brother had missed, Enrico Cortesi also pulled out a gun and took aim at Harry Sabini. Showing great courage, and thinking that Cortesi would never fire at a woman, Louisa ran and intervened between him and his intended victim. Harry Sabini pushed her to one side, allowing Cortesi to fire a shot which hit him in the stomach.

There ensued a general fight during the course of which another member of the Cortesi gang, Alexander Tomaso, attacked Darby Sabini with a bottle, wounding his head and smashing his false teeth. Harry was quickly transported to the Royal Free Hospital, which at that time was in nearby Gray's Inn Road. Though initially not expected to live, he made a full recovery and was able to give evidence at the trial of the Cortesi brothers the following year.

At the trial, Gus and Enrico Cortesi were convicted of attempted murder. The Judge was very lenient and sentenced them to only three years in prison, saying that the reputation of the victims was on a par with that of the accused. However he made a point of praising the courageous behaviour of Louisa Doralli in trying to protect the two victims.

In his evidence to the court, Darby Sabini made clear that he considered the worst aspect of the affair to be the damage that was done to his false teeth.

Easter in 'The Hill'

by Tony Grieco

Stripped of its religious significance, the story of the Passion, Death and Resurrection of Christ is material of great drama, and the wise priests used that drama to put across the religious truths they wished to communicate. Thus the 'Italian Mission' during Lent was born. Priests came from Italy, invited by the clergy of St Peter's Italian Church, to preach heart-rending sermons about the Last Supper, the Way of the Cross or the Sorrows of the Virgin – sermons that were calculated to draw the full range of emotions from the listeners. These preachers were expert orators: one moment they had their congregation hardly daring to breath, the next they had them in floods of tears. They used examples from the people's own lives to show up the greed, sinfulness and inhumanity of man which really crucified Christ. They made the people feel the guilt and taste the vinegar of sorrow before reassuring them that, just as Christ would rise again at Easter, so they too could rise out of their sinfulness with repentance and acceptance of God's love. The appeal of their priests was strong and the church remained packed every night.

It is easy to dismiss these *feverini* for their use of an obvious call to emotions, but remember that, to the people of 'The Hill', emotion ruled all, and that included their religious life. These preachers knew this and they used that knowledge to cultivate the correct attitude at that important feast.

The tears they brought forth from the congregations were not faked – the people really did feel a deep sorrow and love for their dying Saviour and (for that moment at least) they were truly sorry for their many (minor) transgressions. Thus purged and assured that they too would rise again with their Christ, they could go about their daily lives again with a clear conscience – until the next Mission.

It wasn't only the Italian priests who could get this response. For many years the Italian Church was run by English priests with the Italian priests only as helpers. Some of these priests, too, knew how to excite the emotions of their congregations. One in particular – a Father Bannin – was a renowned astronomer who could take his congregation into the biblical Heaven via the wondrous and awe-inspiring mysteries of the visible universe. The language problem meant, however, that, wonderful though Fr Bannin's sermons sounded, most of the immigrants couldn't understand him and more often than not the size of the congregation was due as much to his fame as a preacher amongst the English Catholics from the surrounding area as to the emotion he aroused amongst his

Italian flock. As good as these English priests were the Italians of the Hill preferred their own and their men guided not only the spiritual life of the area but a good deal of its material life too.

I may have given the impression in the preceding paragraphs that Easter was not taken very seriously by the inhabitants of the Hill. That was not what I intended. The simple truth is that many of the Italians were too busy to do more than their duty to this most important of Christian feasts. The reason for this was a matter of pure survival. Easter was the transitional time. Spring had arrived, summer was fast approaching and that meant that ice cream carts, knife grinding equipment and barrel organs must be made ready for the most lucrative period of the year. The weeks of Lent were spent painting the carts and preparing the equipment. Soon after Easter the fairs on the edges of London would attract thousands and our forefathers of the Hill had to be ready to cater for this multitude. Lent and Easter were the time of preparation, the time when winter grime was cleaned off ready for a (hopefully) successful summer. In fact this time of preparation matches very closely the religious feeling of the season.

There is a strong connection between the darkness and despair of mankind before the Resurrection and the revival of local family fortunes in the summer. In their own way, the people lived out the religious truths of Lent and Easter and I'm sure the connection was not lost on the wily preachers of the Mission. By pointing to the lives of the congregation they could explain the deepest truths of Christianity and the true significance of Easter – further proof to the people of how the truth of God worked on the material life of the Hill.

A knife grinder and organ grinder; and an Eyre Street Hill ice-cream vendor

Two well-loved priests
Father Roberto Russo –
the priest with the golden touch

Padre Roberto Russo was born in Rome on 27 August 1930. When he passed away suddenly on 2 April 2001, at the age of 70, the whole congregation of St Peter's Italian Church, not least his friend and colleague Father Carmelo, were bereft. No-one could believe that he had left his flock so suddenly and everyone knew that they had lost a good friend, a saintly man who cared for, and gave all his time to, young and old alike. At his funeral a cloud of sorrow hung over the congregation who were saying goodbye to a man who had encouraged and supported them all in their faith and in their everyday lives. A generous, kind and gentle man, always smiling and laughing, his only weakness was his inability to say 'no' to any request, however impossible.

If you believe God repays us for our good deeds, then that was certainly true of Father Russo. Over a number of years he gained an uncanny reputation for winning raffles, tombolas, the National Lottery and other prizes. He won the first prize in the St Peter's Church raffle, a Fiat car, not once but two years in succession, having previously won the choice between a colour television and a trip to the Bahamas, not to mention over £30,000 in cash over the years. He claimed never to have lost at a game of chance since he arrived in London. There began to be talk of miracles and he himself admitted: 'I enjoy the excitement of winning and I always hope and pray I will win something, big of course!'

Needless to say, Father Russo kept none of his winnings for himself; every penny was given away to the needy whom he encountered in the course of his work as parish priest. He admitted that God could be working through him and firmly believed if he started to keep his winnings to himself, his luck would quickly run out.

Father Carmelo

Father Carmelo Di Giovanni was born in Sangineto, province of Cosenza, on 3 May 1944. His parents were Rosaria and Domenico Di Giovanni. He entered Father Pallottini's Seminary at the age of twelve and eventually graduated in theology at the Lateran University in Rome. He then studied sociology at the University 'La Sapienza', also in Rome, and was finally ordained to the priesthood on 20 December 1970 in the Cathedral of Frascati.

As a young priest he was very active politically and not always in the best of favour with the Church hierarchy. In September 1971 he was transferred to London. He tried to continue his political and social work here but felt at sea in his new, alien environment. For a while he moved to Russia, eventually undergoing a spiritual crisis which completely changed his view of the direction his work should be taking.

Back in London, at St Peter's Italian Church, he became a familiar figure in the local men's prisons, where he befriended the Italian prisoners and helped to point them towards a better life. He always said that he saw the prison as a part of his parish.

In the 1980s there occurred a great influx of young Italians who were addicted to drugs and often suffering from AIDS, and as was to be expected, Father Carmelo did everything in his power to help these desperate young people. His activities with these addicts upset many of his regular parishioners, who thought they would be a bad influence on other young people and children in the parish. Father Carmelo ignored these objections and once a week organised a home-cooked meal in the Priests' House on Back Hill for his 'druggies'.

Father Carmelo

He was an enthusiastic traveller and the list of countries he visited is endless. In 2010, on the 40th anniversary of his ordination, he produced a beautifully illustrated book of photographs of his travels around the world, and of the many famous people he encountered, politicians, presidents, Popes, Mother Teresa and others. With Father Russo, he officiated at the marriage of many young couples, both Italian and British.

Father Carmelo retired to Rome in 2014. He left behind him the great affection and friendship of all his parishioners. Over the years, despite his busy working life, he attended many social gatherings in his community where he was always welcomed by both young and old.

The death of his colleague and friend, Fr Russo, came as a great blow to him, as theirs had been a great working relationship over the years; and the community shared his sorrow.

Fathers Russo and Carmelo

Two well-loved priests

A changing world – Delia's story

Delia's parents, Linda and Dorando Fazzani, spent their early married years in a flat on Bourne Estate, Clerkenwell, living their life in the time-honoured second generation Catholic Italian family style. The couple had three daughters, Delia the youngest was born in 1946. The family later settled in Highbury. In the mid-sixties, a nightmare time for the parents of teenage children, things out there on the young scene were changing rapidly; at this time the generation gap had expanded into a vast chasm.

Delia's parents, Linda and Dorando Fazzani spent their early married years in a flat on teenage children, things out there on the young scene were changing rapidly; at this time the generation gap had expanded into a vast chasm.

When Delia was 18 years old, the unthinkable happened, she found that she was pregnant and the father of the baby denied all responsibility. The poor young girl was terrified. Her father Dorando was a very strict, domineering character and she knew that her mother, even if she was sympathetic, would not dare to go against him. She kept her secret for seven long agonising months, finally, petrified and knowing full well what the outcome would be, she dropped the bombshell. She heard her father rage at the shame and disgrace she was bringing on the family; she was sent away immediately to a mother and baby convent in Epping and was ordered to keep silent about the whole affair, never to mention it to family or friends ever again. She knew that her father would insist on the baby being adopted and that there was not a hope in hell that she would be allowed to keep her. She had no money, no job, no home, and there was no alternative, she had to let the baby go. When the child was six weeks old she was taken away and Delia was left with just a tiny photograph that she had managed to take in secret.

She and her father signed the adoption papers and Delia returned home. Nursing her grief at her loss, alone, not able to talk about the baby or even mention her name, she had given the baby the only thing she could give: a name, Michelle. Delia was heartbroken but she had to suffer in silence. In later years, with a broken heart, she vowed to find her baby and explain to her that it was never her wish to let her go, and how often she had longed to hold her and tell her that she loved her. When Delia made the resolve to one day find her daughter, she never dreamt that it would be so difficult. She made tentative enquiries on her own, but her father would never reveal the name of the couple who had adopted the baby, and when he died in 1977 he took the knowledge with him. No help was forthcoming from the adoption society. There were times when the task seemed impossible but each year, as Michelle's birthday came around, Delia's resolve would strengthen. Even after the death of Dorando, her mother never mentioned the event or the baby again. Until 1991 when her mother Linda's health failed, and learning that her days were numbered and knowing the ordeal that Delia had gone through, Linda begged her to find the baby and insisted that Delia put the only photo they had of the baby on the locker, where she could see it from her bed.

When Delia said that the family were bound to ask questions about the photo, her mother replied that it no longer mattered who knew, and that the priority was for Delia to find her child. Linda had always known in her heart that Delia had never recovered from her loss and she now wanted to put things right. She told her that she remembered a name from the adoption papers and she thought that it must be the name of the adoptive parents. This information gave Delia added incentive, but in the long run it turned out to be the name of the air force base where the family were stationed at the time of the adoption. The search went on; she tried to get information from the convent where the baby had been born, but the only knowledge she was able to extract from them was that the father was an American pilot, stationed in England at the time of the adoption, and that the family had long since returned to America. Delia tried many sources: Cardinal Hume, the Queen, the Citizens' Advice Bureau, St Catherine's House, the American Embassy, the US Airforce, the Salvation Army, and the Public Records Office. Part of the problem was that she had so little information, just the date of the birth, and she had already tried the hospital where Michelle was born. The list is endless. In desperation, she sought publicity; she contacted the *Cilla Black Show*, Anneka Rice, Oprah Winfrey and several others, all to no avail. Finally she contacted an American TV show called *Unsolved Mysteries*. The programme took up the challenge, Delia was flown to Boston and a few days later she sat before the cameras. This was it, her big chance to trace the daughter that she had last seen twenty-seven years ago. They went through the details of the baby's birth and showed the little photo that Delia had cherished for so long. The waiting was not yet over, Delia returned to England. Three months later the show was broadcast all over America. Delia was informed and the agonising wait began. She sat by the phone in agony, supposing she was too late – in twenty-seven years anything could have happened. Thirty minutes after the show went out, the phone rang. She picked it up. 'Your daughter has contacted us and is waiting for your call!'

'Hi, Mom.' Could any words have been sweeter? The long search was over. Mother and daughter talked for almost four hours. Michelle, now Laura Frankland, was married to an American police officer and was the mother of two children.

Delia's long search was over. A meeting was arranged, Delia flew to the USA to meet her daughter, there were no recriminations. Michelle (Laura) fully understood why her mother had had to let her go and she had had a happy and loving home with her adopted family.

The happy ending to Delia's story is that the programme flew her t o America to meet her daughter. As you can imagine, there was a joyous reunion. Delia was later introduced to Charles Power, the pilot who had adopted Michelle, (sadly his wife had died the year before.) When she met the man who had played the role of father to Laura for twenty-seven years, she finally felt that she had not let her baby down. The Powers had adored the baby, and what is more they had been able to give Laura (Michelle) a lifestyle way beyond the means of the young, unworldly girl who had given birth to her.

An important factor in the reunion was that it also helped to lift the deep shame that Delia had been made to feel for so many years. In 1992 Laura arrived in England where Delia threw a big family party for her to meet the whole family. Can you imagine the surprised relatives on hearing the story and meeting their new-found relative, Delia's baby whose birth had been kept such a close secret for so long.

Runnymede 1944 – 1949

Olive Besagni's reminiscences

One Sunday morning with two girl friends from the Cricklewood Skating Club which I had joined at the age of 17, and an old school friend, we set off for a bike ride, my having recently acquired my first bike, bought on the 'h.p.' (hire purchase). As I was working and earning a wage, my parents had conceded to my desire to own a bike – (a) because, on account of the war, there was hardly any traffic on the roads, petrol being rationed, etc; and (b) if I paid for it myself my conduct on the road would be my own responsibility. However, my mother came with me to the shop to ensure that I bought a sensible upright lady's Hercules. The bike cost in the region of £8. I was thrilled anyway. In my eyes it could have been a Rolls Royce – the chrome was gleaming, it had two gears and it was very comfortable. It was spring and the sun was shining, so off we went wearing our cycling shorts, which were pretty short by the standards of the day.

Bruno and his bicycle

My school friend Joyce and I set off from Hampstead and joined Rita and Daphne at Hendon. We cycled onto the North Circular Road with no specific destination in mind, as happy as sandboys, singing *Chattanooga Choo Choo* and other popular songs; and, in between times, moaning about our Mums and Dads who insisted on our returning home by 10.30pm and wouldn't let us go to all night parties, when everyone else's parents didn't mind.

Eventually we found ourselves on the Great West Road where there was the luxury of a cycle path. (You're probably wondering what all this has to do with 'The Hill' – I'm coming to it. We passed a small aerodrome, 'Heath Row' and on through the small town of Staines, where we stopped at a roadside café, a bit of a dump, and indulged in lemonade and a cake. The sense of freedom! The world was our oyster. I noticed there were toilets in the field behind the café, so off we went to repair our make-up. In front of the loos was a cluster of bikes, propped one against the other. A green field edged by trees stretched in front of us, where groups of young people were chatting and sunbathing. Others were playing handball and, despite the heat, groups of boys were playing football. We had discovered Runnymede.

To us girls, this certainly looked, to use a modern phrase, to be 'where it was at'. We investigated further – a river with people swimming; and across the river a small island. When I saw that island I knew I wouldn't be happy until I had returned to Runnymede with my swimming costume and swum across the river for even more investigation.

A party of cyclists at Runnymede

We threw ourselves down on the grass to sunbathe, quite unintentionally of course, near a group of boys and, after the usual banter, they joined us. I had already decided that they looked slightly foreign. It wasn't long before I discovered that they were Anglo-Italian teenagers, boys whose families had originated from *Il Quartiere* or the surrounding districts. Although I didn't know them personally, I knew families that they knew, families whose acquaintance I had made during the years I worked at Pagliai's, the statuette makers off Goswell Road.

We returned home with red, sunburnt knees, exhausted but exhilarated and determined to return soon. My friends were not taken with the exhausting pastime of cycling and so remained faithful to Cricklewood Skating Rink. But henceforth I could think of nothing other than returning to Runnymede. For the next three years, on the first fine day of spring, I would polish up my bike and head for Windsor.

Sometimes I would set off alone but it wouldn't be long before I would meet up with one or several of the lads from the *Quartiere* who, like me with the first breath of spring, had only one thing on their mind: Runnymede.

It was innocent fun but, Italian lads being what they were, at the sight of a pretty girl the cry would go up: 'To the woods!' I must say it was all bravado, and the fun was the fresh air and companionship. I swam over to the island many times during those halcyon days. One of the attractions was a dilapidated villa with what had once been a swimming pool, now full of rubbish, leaves and broken tiles, but it still smacked of the opulence that must have existed before the war. I used to imagine who had been the lucky people who had used that place as a holiday home. Apart from having quite a strong undercurrent at times, the river could be pretty cold, but there were diving boards and a shallow section where children could paddle. So we indulged in tomatoes on fried bread and cycled home, sometimes thirty-strong, swinging round Piccadilly Circus singing *Quel Mazzolin di Fiori* to the amusement, or often dismay, of the passers-by.

As well as the lads from Clerkenwell, the West End Italians had also caught the cycling to Runnymede bug. The difference between the two groups was marked by the latter owning obviously expensive bikes and the latest cycling apparel, whereas the boys from the Hill would be riding anything that had two wheels, some of them wearing cut-down trousers for shorts. If anything, it was they who were having all the fun, but there was hardly any animosity between the two groups. If someone had a puncture or their bike had broken down, everyone would come to the rescue; sometimes a group would spend hours giving attention to some unfortunate's snapped gears or other problems.

Eventually the war ended and traffic on the roads increased. Some of the couples who had met at Runnymede were now married. Bruno and I were wed in 1948 and the tandem that we had acquired by then was sold. The space in the hallway that had accommodated it was given over to our first baby daughter Anita's 'Marmet' pram.

Olive and Bruno: in place of their tandem, a pram

Afterword

This year, 2015, my husband Bruno and I will both be celebrating our 90th birthdays. It is my belief that Bruno, the oldest son of the Besagni family, is one of the few remaining Italians who were born and grew up 'down the Hill'. We now have three children, Anita, Tony and Nicolette, seven grandsons and a granddaughter, Leah, who recently presented us with our first great-grandchild, a girl, Gaby. Time to conclude my story. ***Ciao!***

Olive Besagni — What a Life!

Olive was born to Jeanetta and Joseph Ferrari on 23 September 1925 in Gospel Oak. She was the youngest of five children and her childhood was one of singing, tap dancing, roller skating at Ally Pally and swimming at Parliament Hill Lido.

Olive's family were a meeting of traditional English – the Oxleys – and the more flamboyant Italian – the Ferraris. Olive as the youngest was thoroughly spoilt by her older brothers and sisters. Sport and music played a major part in all their lives and at the centre of it was St Dominic's Priory Youth Club and choir.

As a 14-year-old girl Londoner Olive was evacuated as war broke out and was sent to Exton in Rutland, which for her was a very happy place and the fact that she put on a play there was probably to start her lifelong passion for am-dram.

Olive did well at school, excelling in English and progressed to the Central School from Fleet Primary.

In 1941 whilst working at Pagliai's of Great Sutton Street, a company that specialised in the traditional method of making religious statues, Olive first glimpsed the man who she would spend the rest of her life with. Her job, which consisted of painting gold lines and lace on the figures, was the first time that Olive had encountered Italian men, even though her grandfather was from Borgotaro and was a well-known teacher of English and a popular person in the Italian community.

After the war Olive landed a job at Realist Films as a trainee negative cutter and then became an assistant film editor. She would later move to Pathé Films which was then a major company in Wardour Street. Olive thrived at Pathé and embraced the film industry culture.

Her romance with Bruno was founded initially on their mutual love of cycling. The gang from 'Down the Hill' regularly cycled to Runnymede and it was during these excursions that love blossomed.

Olive and Bruno married in July 1948, a wonderful white wedding at St Peter's. Olive and Bruno lived initially at Constantine Road but by 1949 they would exchange their tandem for a pram at the birth of their daughter Anita. They then moved to Montpelier Grove in Kentish Town and by 1952 their son Anthony was born. Olive never settled in that house and in 1956 they would make a move that would prove to be more than just a flat at Myddelton Square, Islington, but a new phase of their life.

Family had been such an integral part of Olive's life but Myddelton Square put Olive and Bruno at the heart of a community and created lifelong friendships. Shortly after they moved to Myddelton Square, Olive resumed her passion for drama when she joined St Peter's and Paul's drama group, where she performed and wrote many memorable shows.

In 1965 an unexpected Christmas present arrived in the shape of their third child Nicolette. It was during the 1960s that both Olive and Bruno became more involved in the Mazzini-Garibaldi club and their social life revolved around club events and dinner dances. The Italian Procession was a big part of her life, walking in the Procession whilst Bruno created magnificent floats and of course there was the annual *Scampagnata*.

Workwise, Olive now in her fifties, reinvented herself and did a business and secretarial course which led to a job at a book publishers', and she later went on to work at the media resources department of Kingsway College.

In the 1980s Olive had started her own drama group and from having been a performer, she now developed her writing and directing skills and produced the shows *Blitz and Pieces*, *Frothy Coffee* and *Down the Hill*. These shows became part of the community and gave an opportunity for the children of family and friends to participate in something really special. On top of all this, somehow she was also running the choir at St Peter's and St Paul's.

Olive was a wonderful mother to Anita, Tony and Nicky and she then became a wonderful mother-in-law to her children's spouses Jack, Marion and Giovanni. A caring grandmother to Steven, Leah, Michael, John Joe, Nicholas, Andrei, Gianni and Luca and finally the joy of being a great grandmother 'Biz Nonna' to Gaby.

Olive's legacy to all of us has been that at the grand old age of 86 she put together a collection of oral histories telling the stories of Italian families in Clerkenwell going back over generations; the book was called *A Better Life*.

In September 2015 Olive and Bruno celebrated their 90th Birthdays. No-one could quite believe that over 100 people who spanned generations all came to sing, dance and celebrate with their favourite Italian couple. It was a real tribute to all the lives that she had touched that she got to celebrate so happily with everyone she loved.

Sadly, in the early hours of Monday, 12 December 2016 Olive turned to Bruno and said 'I want to go home', she closed her eyes and peacefully went. That day the world lost one of its brightest stars. Unforgettable. Irreplaceable. Forever in our hearts.

Olive on her 91st birthday

The Besagni family in 2010

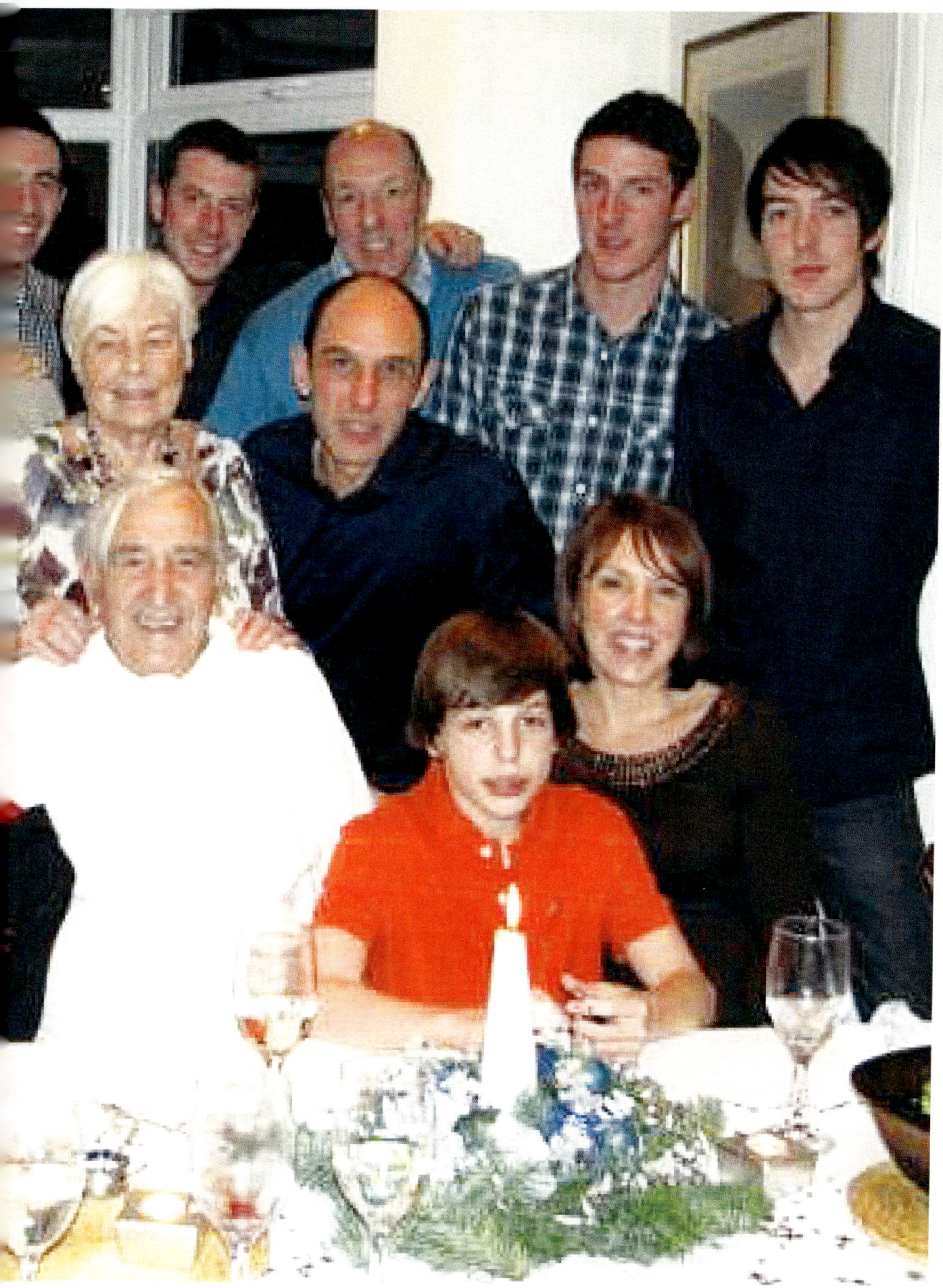

Index

* = illustration(s)

A

Abate, Rosa 10
Abel, Brother 23
Agnes, Sister 47, 48
Albion Buildings 31
Albion Street 10
Amoroso, Fr 33
Amwell Street 50
Anthony, Cav Fr 22
Antonioni, Maria 47*
Arlecchiono Players 33
Army, see British...; Italian...
Arnaud, of Caraglio 42
Arsenal FC 19
asphalt trade 13

B

Back Hill 20, 22, 31, 33, 42, 50, 56
Backhill (magazine) 39, 43
Bacuzzi, Joe 18-19*
Bailey, Mr 22
Bakers Row 9, 23
Balfe Street 10
Ballestrina, Sig.na 21
Balsamo (barber) 21
Balzani, Patrizia 25
bands 23
Bannin, Fr 53
barbers 21, 23, 35
barrel organs 21, 54*
Bastiani, Gino 35
Bath Street, see Great Bath Street
Bazzini family 68, 71*
Bella Venezia restaurant 40
Belli, Tina 24
Bennelli, Mr 12
Bergomini's 23
'Bersaglieri' 39, 40, 41
Bertoncini, Peter 32-33*
Besagni family
  Bruno 15, 37, 44*, 61*, 63*, 65, 66
  Dorina 73*
  Olive 6, 7*, 15, 24, 61-63, 65-66, 67*
Bonomi family 15
Bourne Estate 47, 58
Bowling Green Lane 27
Boyne, Katherine 34
Bracchi, Luisa 24
British Army, *service in* 9, 10*, 19
Bruschini, Mrs 21

C

Café Royal 36
Caledonian Road 26
Caliendo, Giuseppe 23
Canale, Gianna Maria 36
Capella, Rita 38
Capocci (barber) 23
Capocci, Mary 21
Caruso, Enrico 42
Casey, Mr 21
Catholicism 53-54; *see also* St Peter's ...; Procession
Cavalca, Irene 31
Cavendish Mansions 10, 12, 14
Central Club 21, 45
Charlotte Street 16
Chiaponcelli, Fr 21, 23
Chiappa & Co. 21
Children of Mary 11, 33
Christmas 21, 36, 49
Cicco family 8-14*
Ciccone family 39, 40
Ciccone & Santella 23
cinema-going 21, 49
Clerici, Natalina 18
Clerini's 23
Clerkenwell Road 10, 12*, 14, 15, 21, 22*, 23, 42, 43
Clerkenwell Screws 12*
Coach & Horses *PH* 19, 50
  outing 57*
Constantine Road 65
Coronation (George VI) 46, 47
Cortesi brothers 52
Crescitelli, Fr 13, 20, 23
Cuffley (Herts.) 11-12
cycling 61-63*, 65

D

Daily Mirror 20
Dainese, Angelo 43-44
Dalston 17
Delaney, Mr 20, 45
De Marco family 50
Di Giovanni, Fr Carmelo 55-57*
Di Giuseppe (barber) 35
Di Troia, Sig.na 40
Doralli, Louisa 37
drama 21, 33, 66
Driscoll, Mr 21

E

Easter/Holy Week 21, 23, 33, 36, 53-54
Edgar, Imelda 26
Ely Place 15
Empire Day 21
evacuation, *see under* World War Two
Exmouth Market 31, 49, 50
Eyre Street Hill 9, 21, 23, 39, 48

F

Fabrizi, Mario 34*
Faccini, Mrs 23
Fackler, Mr 21
Falca's water factory 23
Falco, Natalie 51
Farringdon Road 18, 20, 35
Fazzani family 58-60
Ferrari family 6, 65
Finsbury Mortuary 29*
Finsbury Town Hall 21
Fleet Primary School 65
football 18-19*, 28*, 37
Forte, Lord Charles 36
Franchi, Miranda 48
Fratellanza Club 52
Freemasons 36
Frewell House 47
Fulham FC 19

G

Gallantry, Mr 25*
Garibaldi, Giuseppe 35*
Gatti, Carlo 20, 39
Gauthier, of Saluzzo 42

70

Gazeley, Lt E 37
Gazzani family 6
Gazzano's 507
Gella's 20
George Yard 42
Giacon, Giovanna 33
Gigatti's 15
Gigli, Beniamino 42
Giovanelli family 24-26*
Globe cinema 21, 49
Goddard, Mr 21
Gospel Oak 65
Goswell Road 23, 51, 62
Gough, Fr 22
Gray's Inn 47
Gray's Inn Road 30, 50, 52
Great Bath Street 2*, 40, 50, 52
Great Percy Street 50
Great Sutton Street 65
Great Windmill Street 24
Grieco family 11-14*
Griffin Mansions 21

H

Hackney Marshes 21, 46
Hadley Woods 47
Haines, Fr 22
Harris's 22
Harvey & Thompson 22
Hastings 22
Hatton Wall 42
Hearn, Patsy 21
Hedderman, Fr 22
Henry, Mr 23
Herbal Hill, *see*
  Little Saffron Hill
Highbury 58
Holborn Borough Council 46, 47
Holborn Fish Restaurant 15
Holborn Town Hall 21
Holborn Tube Station 47
Holloway 11
Hornchurch 37
Hunter Penrose 20

I

ice cream trade 23,
  39, 40, 48, 54*
ice trade 20, 39, 40*

immigration 8-9
internment, 9, *22*
Irish community 11, 27
Italian Army, *service in* 9*
'Italian Missions' 23, 53-54
Italian Operatives' Society 35
Italian Procession, *see* Procession

ITALY (*place names arranged*
  by region and province)
Calabria
  Cosenza: Sangineto 55
Campania
  Naples 8
    Nola 8, 10, 12
    Salerno: Salvitelle 11
Emilia Romagna
  Parma 26
    Bardi 26
      Gravago
      Grezzo 24, 26
      Cacrovoli 26
    Piacenza 35
      Bettola 25
      Chiavenna Rocchetta 15
Lazio
  Picinisco 39
  Rome 55
Liguria: Genoa 43
Lombardy: Milan 18, 43
Tuscany
  Florence 25
  Lucca 33
  Massa-Carrara
    Bratto 17
    Cinquale 30
Veneto: Treviso 26

J

James, Brother 21
Johnson Matthey 23
Jones's Dairy 23

K

Kelly, Fr 22
Kennedy, Fr 21
Kensal Green 14, 34
Kibble, A.W. (Victor) 27-30

King's Cross 10, 11, 24

Tube Station: fire 57
King's Cross Road 18, 39
Kingsway College 66
Kingsway Hall 21
Kingsway Institute 47
knife grinders 54*

L

Lamb, Fr 21
Langdon, Ald. 46
La Sainte Union 38
Laurati family 21
Laystall Street 21, 35
Leape, Miss 21
Leather Lane 22, 31
Lebaldi, Beo 31*
Leicester Place 20, 23
Lent 53-54
Liriosi's 23
Little California 37, 38*
Little Italy (*in general*) 6
Little Saffron Hill 20, 42
Lloyd & Sons 22*, 23
Lollobrigida, Gina 36
London County Council 47
London Ice Cream Assoc. 39, 40
Lusardi family 15-17*
Lynsky, Jack 21

M

McKee, Mr 21, 25*, 45
MacVay, Miss 20
Malangone, Amelia 21
Mancini, Antonio 41
Manze's 49
Marcantoni, Miranda 40
Mariani's 50
Mazzini, Giuseppe 35*
Mazzini-Garibaldi
  Club 9, 11, 26, 35-38*, 66
  Foundation 37
Mazzochi, Maria 25
Metropolitan *PH* 22
Mildner, F. & Co 21
Miller-Bryson, Sir John 41
Monmouth 26
Monte, Carmela 50
Montpelier Grove 65
mortuary 29*

71

Murtagh, F.V. 21, 45, 47
Myddelton Square 65

N
Nazzani family 15-17
Neasden 34
Necchi, Lou 26
Neville, Mrs 30
Newgate Street (Herts.) 12
Nolan, Charles 20-23
North Hyde Boys Band 23
Northampton Road 29
Northdown Street 24
Notaro, Mrs T. 48

O
organ grinder 54*
Our Lady of Mount
 Carmel, see Procession
Oxley family 6, 65

P
Pagliai, O. Ltd 52, 65
Pallottine Fathers 41, 55
Panizzi, Antonio 44
Parliament Hill Lido 65
Pathé 65
Patterson, Rt Rev. W.L. 42
Paulini, Joseph 46
pawnbrokers 30
Perella family 39, 41
picnics 37-38*
Pini, Serafino 35
play 22, 23, 29*
Pompa, Achille 39*
prisoners of war 11-12
Procession 2*, 13, 21, 22*,
 26, 29, 32*, 33, 49, 66
Proctor, Miss 2

Q
Quaradagini, Lino 35

R
Rech, Gemma 26
Red Lion Street 26, 35
Regali Bros 21
Rhesteghini, Lou 50
Ricordi family 16
Roberto's 23
Roman Catholicism 53-54; see
 also St Peter's ...; Procession
Rosebery Avenue 33
Royal Air Force 30
Royal Free Hospital 46, 52
Runnymede 61-63*, 65
Russo, Fr Roberto 55-57*

S
Sabini, Darby 52*
St Dominic's Priory 65
St Peter's Boys' Club 21, 26
St Peter's Dramatic Club 21
St Peter's Italian Church 8, 13, 19,
 20, 21, 22, 26, 27, 33, 41-42*,
 53-54
 clergy 21, 22, 23, 55-57*
 marriages 12, 13, 59, 65
 priests' house 33, 56
St Peter's Italian School 9, 20, 21
 diary 45-47
 football team 28*
 pupils 9, 20, 21, 24, 25*, 27,
  28*, 34, 44*, 46*, 47*, 48, 50
 staff 6, 9, 20, 21, 25*, 28, 44,
  45*, 47*
SS Peter & Paul Church 142, 143
Santini, Bessie 50
Scampagnata (picnic) 37-38*, 66
Secchi, Frank 50
Secchi, Mamie 50-51
Sedgwick, Miranda 48-49
Silveri, Paolo 20
singing 37, 40, 63
Smithfield 39
Soho 24, 40, 50, 65
Spa Fields 29*, 46

statuette trade 13, 21, 65
Stauder, Mme 39
Steel, Sally 26
Stevenson, Mr 21, 46
street musicians 23, 41, 54*
Summer Street 9
Suttons (Essex) 37
'Swing Gardens' 29*
Swiss Club 15

T
Taylor, John 9
terrazzo trade 24
Terroni's 50
Tomaso, Alexander 52
Topham Street 40
tortoises 31*

V
Valente, Alessandro 40
Vickers & Sons 42
Victoria, Queen 41
Victoria Dwellings 9, 18, 22, 23
Vidor factory 50

W
Wardour Street 65
Warner Street 2*, 21, 23, 33, 52
Wharton Street 50
Wheeler, Mr 22
Whiskin Street 24
Wild Street School 22
Wilmington Square 50
Wiseman, Cardinal 41
Wootton Bassett 21, 47, 50
World War One 9, 10
World War Two
 evacuation 11, 21, 47, 50, 65
 internment 9, 22
 POWs 11-12

YZ
Yardley Street 50
Zanelli, Mary 50

Two more images of the annual Procession: from the 1930s (girls led by Dorina Besagni), and from the 1990s